INTELLIGENCE AND COUNTERINTELLIGENCE STUDIES

NSA INTELLIGENCE COLLECTION, LEAKS, AND THE PROTECTION OF CLASSIFIED INFORMATION

BACKGROUND AND ISSUES

Intelligence and Counterintelligence Studies

Additional books in this series can be found on Nova's website under the Series tab.

Additional E-books in this series can be found on Nova's website under the E-book tab.

INTELLIGENCE AND COUNTERINTELLIGENCE STUDIES

NSA INTELLIGENCE COLLECTION, LEAKS, AND THE PROTECTION OF CLASSIFIED INFORMATION

BACKGROUND AND ISSUES

SIMON CEPEDA
EDITOR

nova publishers
New York

For permission to use material from this book please contact us:
Telephone 631-231-7269; Fax 631-231-8175
Web Site: http://www.novapublishers.com

Additional color graphics may be available in the e-book version of this book.

Library of Congress Cataloging-in-Publication Data

ISBN: 978-1-62948-937-7

Published by Nova Science Publishers, Inc. † New York

Contents

PREFACE

Media stories about National Security Agency (NSA) surveillance pertain to the unauthorized disclosures of two different intelligence collection programs. These programs arise from provisions of the Foreign Intelligence Surveillance Act (FISA). However, they rely on separate authorities, collect different types of information, and raise different policy questions. This book provides background and issues for Congress with NSA surveillance leaks; provides a primer on some of the fundamental aspects of the security clearance process, using a "frequently asked questions" format; discusses criminal prohibitions on the publication of classified defense information; the legal framework of the protection of classified information; and practices and proposals of the protection of classified information by Congress.

Chapter 1 - Surveillance performed by the National Security Agency (NSA) has received attention for the unauthorized disclosure of two different intelligence collection programs. Since these programs were publicly disclosed over the course of two days in June 2013, there has been confusion about what information is being collected and under which authorities the NSA is acting. This report clarifies the differences between the two programs and identifies potential issues that may help Members of Congress assess legislative proposals pertaining to NSA surveillance authorities.

The first program collects in bulk the phone records—including the number that was dialed from, the number that was dialed to, and the date and duration of the call—of customers of Verizon and possibly other U.S. telephone service providers. It does not collect the content of the calls or the identity of callers. The data are collected pursuant to Section 215 of the USA PATRIOT ACT, which amended the Foreign Intelligence Surveillance Act (FISA) of 1978. Section 215 allows the FBI, in this case on behalf of the NSA, to apply to the Foreign Intelligence Surveillance Court (FISC) for an order compelling a person to produce "any tangible thing," such as records held by a telecommunications provider, if the tangible things sought are "relevant to an authorized investigation." Some commentators have expressed skepticism regarding how such a broad amount of data could be said to be "relevant to an authorized investigation," as required by the statute. In response to these concerns, the Obama Administration subsequently declassified portions of a FISC order authorizing this program and a "whitepaper" describing the Administration's legal reasoning.

The second program targets the electronic communications, including content, of foreign targets overseas whose communications flow through American networks. These data are collected pursuant to Section 702 of FISA, which was added by the FISA Amendments Act of 2008. This program acquires information from Internet service providers, as well as through what NSA terms "upstream" collection that appears to acquire Internet traffic while it is in transit from one location to another. Although this program targets the communications of foreigners who are abroad, the Administration has acknowledged that technical limitations in the "upstream" collection result in the collection of some communications that are unrelated to the target or that may take place between persons in the United States. Notwithstanding these technical limitations, the FISC has held that this program is consistent with the requirements of both Section 702 and the Fourth Amendment provided that there are sufficient safeguards in place to identify and limit the retention, use, or dissemination of such unrelated or wholly domestic communications.

The Obama Administration has argued that these surveillance activities, in addition to being subject to oversight by all three branches of government, are important to national security and have helped disrupt terror plots. These arguments have not always distinguished between the two programs, and some critics, while acknowledging the value of information collected using Section 702 authorities, are skeptical of the value of the phone records held in bulk at NSA. Thus, recent legislative proposals have primarily focused on modifying Section 215 to preclude the breadth of phone records collection currently taking place. They have also emphasized requiring greater public disclosure of FISC opinions, including the opinion(s) allowing for the collection of phone records in bulk.

This report discusses the specifics of these two NSA collection programs. It does not address other questions that have been raised in the aftermath of these leaks, such as the potential harm to national security caused by the leaks or the intelligence community's reliance on contractors.

Chapter 2 – This report provides a primer on some of the fundamental aspects of the security clearance process, using a "Frequently Asked Questions" format.

A security clearance is a determination that an individual—whether a direct federal employee or a private contractor performing work for the government—is eligible for access to classified national security information. A security clearance alone does not grant an individual access to classified materials. Rather, a security clearance means that an individual is eligible for access. In order to gain access to specific classified materials, an individual should also have a demonstrated "need to know" the information contained in the specific classified materials.

There are three levels of security clearances: Confidential, Secret, and Top Secret, which correspond to the levels of sensitivity of the information that a cleared individual will be eligible to access. In addition, there are two major categories of classified information that are commonly associated with the Top Secret level: Sensitive Compartmented Information (SCI), which refers to intelligence sources and methods, and Special Access Programs (SAPs), which refers to highly sensitive policies, projects, and programs. These categories exist for classified information that has been deemed particularly vulnerable. Eligibility standards and investigative requirements for access to SCI and SAPs are higher than for access to information otherwise classified at the same level, which further restricts the number of individuals eligible for access.

Federal employees and private contractors must be cleared in order to gain access to classified materials. An individual may not obtain or initiate a security clearance on his or her own. A sponsoring federal agency initiates the process and will make the final security clearance determination based on a background investigation.

Although the process involves a number of stages, four key steps to obtaining and maintaining a security clearance are (1) agency sponsorship and submission of clearance application materials; (2) a background investigation, the extent of which may vary by level of clearance; (3) an adjudication to determine whether an individual will be deemed eligible for access; and (4) periodic reinvestigations. Adjudication and final clearance determinations are generally made by the sponsoring agency. To maintain a security clearance, an individual is also subject to periodic reinvestigations. The frequency of reinvestigations vary by level of clearance.

The Office of Personnel Management, Federal Investigative Services (OPM-FIS) oversees approximately 90% of all background investigations. Typically, the costs of a background investigation, including background investigations of private contractors, are paid for by the requesting agency. While the final determination to grant or deny a security clearance is typically made by the requesting agency, with certain exceptions a security clearance granted by one agency may be accepted by other agencies. It is difficult, however, to determine the degree to which reciprocity occurs between agencies.

Chapter 3 - The publication of classified information related to National Security Agency (NSA) surveillance activity is the latest in a series of leaks to the press that has riveted Congress's attention. Press reports describing classified U.S. operations abroad have led to calls from Congress for an investigation into the source of the leaks, and Attorney General Holder appointed two special prosecutors to look into the matter. The online publication of classified defense documents and diplomatic cables by the organization WikiLeaks and subsequent reporting by the *New York Times* and other news media had already focused attention on whether such publication violates U.S. criminal law. The source of the WikiLeaks material, Army Private Bradley Manning, has been sentenced to 35 years' imprisonment for a number of offenses under the Uniform Code of Military Justice (UCMJ), but was not convicted of aiding the enemy. A grand jury in Virginia is deciding whether to indict any civilians in connection with the disclosure. A number of other cases involving charges under the Espionage Act, including efforts to extradite Edward Snowden in connection with the leak of NSA documents pertaining to certain surveillance programs, demonstrate the Obama Administration's relatively hardline policy with respect to the prosecution of persons suspected of leaking classified information to the media.

This report identifies some criminal statutes that may apply to the publication of classified defense information, noting that these have been used almost exclusively to prosecute individuals with access to classified information (and a corresponding obligation to protect it) who make it available to foreign agents, or to foreign agents who obtain classified information unlawfully while present in the United States. While prosecutions appear to be on the rise, leaks of classified information to the press have relatively infrequently been punished as crimes, and we are aware of no case in which a publisher of information obtained through unauthorized disclosure by a government employee has been prosecuted for publishing it. There may be First Amendment implications that would make such a prosecution difficult, not to mention political ramifications based on concerns about government censorship. To the extent that the investigation implicates any foreign nationals whose conduct occurred entirely overseas, any resulting prosecution may carry foreign policy implications related to the exercise of extraterritorial jurisdiction and whether suspected persons may be extradited to the United States under applicable treaty provisions.

This report discusses the statutory prohibitions that may be implicated, including the Espionage Act; the extraterritorial application of such statutes; and the First Amendment implications related to such prosecutions against domestic or foreign media organizations and associated individuals. The report provides a summary of previous legislative efforts to criminalize the unauthorized disclosure of classified information.

Chapter 4 - This report provides an overview of the relationship between executive and legislative authority over national security information, and summarizes the current laws that form the legal framework protecting classified information, including current executive orders and some agency regulations pertaining to the handling of unauthorized disclosures of classified information by government officers and employees. The report also summarizes criminal laws that pertain specifically to the unauthorized disclosure of classified information, as well as civil and administrative penalties. Finally, the report describes some recent developments in executive branch security policies and relevant legislative activity.

Chapter 5 - The protection of classified national security and other controlled information is of concern not only to the executive branch—which, for the most part, determines what information is classified and controlled—but also to Congress. The legislature uses such information to fulfill its constitutional responsibilities, particularly overseeing the executive, appropriating funds, and legislating public policy. Congress has established numerous mechanisms to safeguard controlled information in its custody, although these arrangements have varied over time, between the two chambers, and among offices in each. Both chambers, for instance, have created offices of security to consolidate relevant responsibilities; but these were established nearly two decades apart. Other differences exist at the committee level, regarding the availability and use of information in committees' custody. Proposals for change, some of which are controversial and could be costly, usually seek to set uniform standards or heighten requirements for access.

In: NSA Intelligence Collection, Leaks … ISBN: 978-1-62948-937-7
Editor: Simon Cepeda

Chapter 1

NSA SURVEILLANCE LEAKS: BACKGROUND AND ISSUES FOR CONGRESS*

John W. Rollins and Edward C. Liu

SUMMARY

Surveillance performed by the National Security Agency (NSA) has received attention for the unauthorized disclosure of two different intelligence collection programs. Since these programs were publicly disclosed over the course of two days in June 2013, there has been confusion about what information is being collected and under which authorities the NSA is acting. This report clarifies the differences between the two programs and identifies potential issues that may help Members of Congress assess legislative proposals pertaining to NSA surveillance authorities.

The first program collects in bulk the phone records—including the number that was dialed from, the number that was dialed to, and the date and duration of the call—of customers of Verizon and possibly other U.S. telephone service providers. It does not collect the content of the calls or the identity of callers. The data are collected pursuant to Section 215 of the USA PATRIOT ACT, which amended the Foreign Intelligence Surveillance Act (FISA) of 1978. Section 215 allows the FBI, in this case on behalf of the NSA, to apply to the Foreign Intelligence Surveillance Court (FISC) for an order

* This is an edited, reformatted and augmented version of the Congressional Research Service Publication, CRS Report for Congress R43134, dated September 4, 2013.

compelling a person to produce "any tangible thing," such as records held by a telecommunications provider, if the tangible things sought are "relevant to an authorized investigation." Some commentators have expressed skepticism regarding how such a broad amount of data could be said to be "relevant to an authorized investigation," as required by the statute. In response to these concerns, the Obama Administration subsequently declassified portions of a FISC order authorizing this program and a "whitepaper" describing the Administration's legal reasoning.

The second program targets the electronic communications, including content, of foreign targets overseas whose communications flow through American networks. These data are collected pursuant to Section 702 of FISA, which was added by the FISA Amendments Act of 2008. This program acquires information from Internet service providers, as well as through what NSA terms "upstream" collection that appears to acquire Internet traffic while it is in transit from one location to another. Although this program targets the communications of foreigners who are abroad, the Administration has acknowledged that technical limitations in the "upstream" collection result in the collection of some communications that are unrelated to the target or that may take place between persons in the United States. Notwithstanding these technical limitations, the FISC has held that this program is consistent with the requirements of both Section 702 and the Fourth Amendment provided that there are sufficient safeguards in place to identify and limit the retention, use, or dissemination of such unrelated or wholly domestic communications.

The Obama Administration has argued that these surveillance activities, in addition to being subject to oversight by all three branches of government, are important to national security and have helped disrupt terror plots. These arguments have not always distinguished between the two programs, and some critics, while acknowledging the value of information collected using Section 702 authorities, are skeptical of the value of the phone records held in bulk at NSA. Thus, recent legislative proposals have primarily focused on modifying Section 215 to preclude the breadth of phone records collection currently taking place. They have also emphasized requiring greater public disclosure of FISC opinions, including the opinion(s) allowing for the collection of phone records in bulk.

This report discusses the specifics of these two NSA collection programs. It does not address other questions that have been raised in the aftermath of these leaks, such as the potential harm to national security caused by the leaks or the intelligence community's reliance on contractors.

INTRODUCTION

Media stories about National Security Agency (NSA) surveillance pertain to the unauthorized disclosures of two different intelligence collection programs. These programs arise from provisions of the Foreign Intelligence Surveillance Act (FISA). However, they rely on separate authorities, collect different types of information, and raise different policy questions. As such, where possible, the information contained in this report distinguishes between the two. For both programs, there is a tension between the speed and convenience with which the government can access data of possible intelligence value and the mechanisms intended to safeguard civil liberties. The first program collects and stores in bulk domestic phone records that some argue could be gathered to equal effect through more focused records requests. The second program targets the electronic communications of non-U.S. persons[1] while they are abroad, but also collects some communications unrelated to those targets.

The following sections address (1) what information is being collected; (2) the legal basis for the collection; (3) existing oversight mechanisms; and (4) arguments for and against the two programs. The last section of this report discusses legislation that has been proposed in response to information disclosed about NSA surveillance. Because documents leaked to the news media may be classified, CRS is precluded from providing a detailed analysis of the content of those documents. The information in this report is based largely on public comments from intelligence officials and Members of Congress.

WHAT INFORMATION IS BEING COLLECTED?

Domestic Collection of Domestic Phone Records—collected under Section 215 of the USA PATRIOT ACT: On Wednesday, June 5, 2013, *The Guardian* reported that NSA collects in bulk the telephone records of millions of U.S. customers of Verizon, pursuant to an order from the Foreign Intelligence Surveillance Court (FISC).[2] Intelligence officials and leaders of the congressional intelligence committees have confirmed the existence of this domestic phone records collection program, although they have not identified the companies providing the records. It has been alleged, but not confirmed, that similar orders have been sent to other telecommunications providers.[3] The court order disclosed by *The Guardian* was a three-month extension of a program that has been going on for seven years.[4] The Director of National Intelligence (DNI) has acknowledged the breadth of the program, analogizing it to "a huge library with literally millions of volumes of books," but has stated that data about Americans in the possession of the United States government can only be accessed under specific circumstances.[5]

The program collects "metadata"—a term used in this context to refer to data about a phone call, but not the phone conversation itself.[6] Intelligence officials have stated that the data are limited to the number that was dialed from, the number that was dialed to, and the date and duration of the call.[7] The data do not include cell site location information. Intelligence officials have committed to alerting Members of Congress before collecting that location information, suggesting they currently have the authority to do so.[8] The data must be destroyed within five years of acquisition.[9] Information collected does not include the location of the call (beyond the area code identified in the phone number), the content of the call, or the identity of the subscriber.[10] However, some civil liberties advocates have argued that a telephone number today is essentially a unique identifier that can be easily tied to a person's identity by other means and that the distinction between a telephone number and subscriber identity is therefore insignificant.

On June 27, 2013, *The Guardian* published an article alleging that NSA previously collected the metadata for Internet-based communications (email being the prime example) for Americans inside the United States.[11] A spokesman for the DNI confirmed *The Guardian*'s account, but said this program was discontinued in 2011. Intelligence officials have stated that, pursuant to the same FISA authorities, NSA does not currently collect in bulk the metadata of these types of communications.[12] The collection of Internet metadata was based on separate FISA authorities.[13] Some have expressed concern that those authorities could again be used to collect Internet metadata in the future.[14]

Domestic Collection of Foreign Internet-Related Data—collected under Section 702 of FISA: *The Washington Post* reported on June 6th, 2013, that, "The National Security Agency and the FBI are tapping directly into the central servers of nine leading U.S. Internet companies, extracting audio and video chats, photographs, e-mails, documents, and connection logs that enable analysts to track foreign targets."[15] *The Guardian* ran a similar story that same day.[16] These articles referred to a system called PRISM allegedly used to collect this data. Outside commentators and government officials have argued that portions of these stories are inaccurate.[17] Public comments from the Administration indicate this intelligence collection is more targeted in scope than was suggested by these articles, and major technology companies have denied giving the federal government direct access to their servers.

The DNI on June 8, 2013, released a public statement saying, "*The Guardian* and *Washington Post* articles refer to collection of communications pursuant to Section 702 of the Foreign Intelligence Surveillance Act."[18] A fact sheet provided by the DNI stated that PRISM is an internal government computer system used to facilitate access to these communications.[19] In accordance with Section 702, this collection program appears largely to involve the collection of data, including the content of communications, of foreign targets overseas whose emails and other forms of electronic communication flow through networks in the United States.[20]

Compared to the breadth of phone records collection under Section 215, this program is more discriminating in terms of its targets—it is focused on the communications of non-U.S. persons located outside the United States—but broader in terms of the type of information collected. Examples cited by the Administration include the email content of communications with individuals inside the United States, but in those cases the targets of the intelligence collection appear to have been non-U.S. citizens located outside the United States.[21]

The original press articles and more recent stories have suggested NSA monitors or can monitor the vast majority of the world's Internet traffic. NSA has stated that it "touches" only 1.6% of Internet traffic and "selects for review" 0.025% of Internet traffic. These portrayals by both critics and proponents may provide an incomplete account of NSA collection because they incorporate certain assumptions about that collection and about what types of Internet traffic are relevant to the public debate about Section 702 authorities. In August, the Office of the DNI released an October 2011 opinion of the Foreign Intelligence Surveillance Court (FISC) that provided additional insight into the scope and nature of Section 702 collection.

According to the 2011 opinion, NSA collected 250 million Internet communications per year using 702 authorities.[22] Of these communications, 91% were acquired "directly from Internet Service Providers." The opinion did not identify specific providers or describe the means NSA uses to "directly" acquire communications. The other 9% were acquired through what NSA calls "upstream collection," meaning acquisition while Internet traffic is in transit from one unspecified location to another.[23] NSA also has two methods for collecting information about a specific target; "to/from" communications collection, in which the target is the sender or receiver of the Internet communications; and "about" communications collection, in which the target is mentioned in the communications of non-targets.[24] "About" communications are acquired through upstream collection.[25] Because this method does not collect the communications to or from specific individuals but rather communications that mention those individuals, it implicates a potentially broader swath of communications and raises additional civil liberties concerns.

What Are the Legal Bases for the Collection?

Domestic Phone Records: Section 215 of the USA PATRIOT ACT,[26] which is the authority under which the collection of domestic phone records has been authorized,[27] broadened government access to private business records by both enlarging the scope of materials that may be sought and lowering the legal standard required to be met.[28] Specifically, Section 215 modified the business records provisions of FISA to allow the FBI to apply to the FISC for an order compelling a person to produce "any tangible thing," including records held by a telecommunications provider concerning the number and length of communications, but not the contents of those communications.[29] In 2005, the provision was further amended to require the FBI to provide a statement of facts showing that there are "reasonable grounds to believe" that the tangible things sought are "relevant to an authorized investigation (other than a threat assessment)" into foreign intelligence, international terrorism, or espionage.[30]

The phrase "reasonable grounds to believe" is not defined by FISA, but has been used interchangeably with the "reasonable suspicion" standard, a less stringent standard than "probable cause."[31] Although there are not any publicly available judicial opinions interpreting this language in the context of Section 215, it may be helpful to look at appellate courts' interpretations of the Stored Communications Act (SCA), as it similarly authorizes law enforcement to access telecommunications transactional records (as well as stored electronic communications) upon a showing that "there are reasonable grounds to believe" that the information sought is "relevant and material to an ongoing criminal investigation."[32] Under the SCA, the collection of stored email has been held to meet that standard in the context of a "complex, large-scale mail and wire fraud operation" in which "interviews of current and former employees of the target company suggest that electronic mail is a vital communication tool that has been used to perpetuate the fraudulent conduct" and "various sources [have verified] that [the provider who had custody of the email] provides electronic communications services to certain individual(s) [under] investigation."[33] Similarly, obtaining the internet protocol (IP) address[34] and name associated with a Yahoo! account was justified when a police officer received a tip from an individual that he had received what appeared to be child pornography from that Yahoo! account.[35]

"Relevancy" is also not defined by FISA, but is generally understood to be a less stringent standard than probable cause requiring only that the information sought would tend to prove or disprove a fact at issue.[36] In August 2013, the Obama Administration released a whitepaper providing a legal analysis of the bulk collection of telephony metadata under Section 215.[37] Included in this whitepaper was an examination of the term "relevancy" as used in Section 215. The whitepaper first noted previous characterizations of relevancy by the Supreme Court described relevance as encompassing "any matter that bears on, or that reasonably could lead to other matter that could bear on, any issue that is or may be in the case."[38] The whitepaper also noted that courts have upheld requests for "entire repositories of records, even when any particular record is unlikely to directly bear on the matter being investigated, because searching the entire repository is the only feasible means to locate the critical documents."[39] On the other hand, the cases cited in the whitepaper do not appear to involve document requests which are on the same scale as the NSA's collection of domestic telephone records.[40] Nevertheless, in approving the order authorizing the NSA's collection of these records, the FISC must necessarily have agreed that Section 215's relevancy requirement had been satisfied.

An "authorized investigation" must be conducted under guidelines approved by the Attorney General under Executive Order 12333 and may not be conducted of a United States person solely upon the basis of activities protected by the First Amendment.[41] The *Attorney General's Guidelines for FBI Domestic Operations* authorize three levels of investigations: assessments, preliminary investigations, and full investigations. Preliminary investigations require an "allegation or information indicative of possible criminal or national security-threatening activity" before being initiated. Similarly, full investigations require "an articulable factual basis for the investigation that reasonably indicates" the existence of some activity constituting a federal crime, a threat to national security, or foreign intelligence. In contrast, assessments do not require any factual predicate.[42] As Section 215 explicitly requires an authorized investigation "other than a threat assessment," it is likely that Section 215 orders may only be used in conjunction with preliminary or full investigations.

Following the disclosure of the FISC order compelling Verizon to produce large amounts of telephony metadata, some commentators have expressed skepticism regarding how there could be "reasonable grounds to believe" that such a broad amount of data could be said to be "relevant to an authorized investigation," as required by the statute. Although the order has been leaked to various media outlets, other pieces of information that would significantly help inform any understanding of how the legal standard in Section 215 is being applied have not yet been disclosed. Specifically, it is not known what was included in the statement of facts that is required to be submitted as part of the application for a Section 215 order. Similarly, there have not been any widespread disclosures of the manner in which the FISC or FICR is applying the "reasonable grounds to believe" or "relevant to an investigation" standards provided in Section 215.

Foreign Internet-Related Data: Title VII, added by the FISA Amendments Act of 2008, provides additional procedures for the acquisition of foreign intelligence information regarding persons who are believed to be outside of the United States. The DNI has stated that the recently disclosed collection of foreign intelligence information from electronic communication service providers has been authorized under Section 702 of FISA, which specifically concerns acquisitions targeting non-U.S. persons who are overseas.[43]

Prior to the enactment of Section 702, and its predecessor in the Protect America Act of 2007, FISA only authorized sustained electronic surveillance or access to electronically stored communications after the issuance of a FISC order that was specific to the target. The FISC, in authorizing electronic surveillance or a physical search, must find probable cause to believe both (1) that the person targeted by the order is a foreign power or its agent, and (2) that the subject of the search (i.e., the telecommunications or place to be searched) is owned, possessed, or will be used by the target.[44]

Section 702 permits the Attorney General (AG) and the DNI to jointly authorize targeting of persons reasonably believed to be located outside the United States, but is limited to targeting non-U.S. persons. Once authorized, such acquisitions may last for periods of up to one year. Under subsection 702(b) of FISA, such an acquisition is also subject to several limitations. Specifically, an acquisition:

- May not intentionally target any person known at the time of acquisition to be located in the United States;
- May not intentionally target a person reasonably believed to be located outside the United States if the purpose of such acquisition is to target a particular, known person reasonably believed to be in the United States;
- May not intentionally target a U.S. person reasonably believed to be located outside the United States;
- May not intentionally acquire any communication as to which the sender and all intended recipients are known at the time of the acquisition to be located in the United States; and
- Must be conducted in a manner consistent with the Fourth Amendment to the Constitution of the United States.[45]

Acquisitions under Section 702 are also geared towards electronic communications or electronically stored information. This is because the certification supporting the acquisition, discussed in the next section, requires the AG and DNI to attest that, among other things, the acquisition involves obtaining information from or with the assistance of an electronic communication service provider.[46] This would appear to encompass acquisitions using methods such as wiretaps or intercepting digital communications, but may also include accessing stored communications or other data.

Central components of Section 702 are the targeting and minimization procedures that must be submitted to the FISC for approval. In order to be approved, Section 702 requires the targeting procedures be reasonably designed to ensure that an acquisition is limited to targeting persons reasonably believed to be located outside the United States, and to prevent the intentional acquisition of any communication where the sender and all intended recipients are known at the time of the acquisition to be located in the United States.[47]

The Fourth Amendment to the U.S. Constitution protects against "unreasonable searches and seizures."[48] In domestic criminal law investigations, it generally requires law enforcement officers to obtain a court-issued warrant before conducting a search.[49] When the warrant requirement does not apply, government activity is generally subject to a "reasonableness" test under the Fourth Amendment.[50] The extent to which the warrant requirement applies to the government's collection of foreign intelligence is unclear. In a 1972 case, the Supreme Court invalidated warrantless electronic surveillance of *domestic* organizations on Fourth Amendment grounds, despite the government's assertion of a national security rationale.[51] However, it indicated that its conclusion might be different in a future case involving the electronic surveillance of foreign powers or their agents, within or outside the United States.[52]

In August 2013, the Obama Administration partially declassified several opinions of the FISC regarding collection activities under Section 702.[53] The first of these opinions, dated October 3, 2011, dealt with the FISC's evaluation of the targeting and minimization procedures proposed by the government to deal with new information regarding the scope of upstream collection. Specifically, the government had recently discovered that its upstream collection activities had acquired unrelated international communications as well as wholly domestic communications due to technological limitations. After being presented with this new information, the FISC found the proposed minimization procedures to be deficient on statutory[54] and constitutional[55] grounds. With respect to the statutory requirements, the FISC noted that the government's proposed minimization procedures were focused "almost exclusively" on information that an analyst wished to use. Consequently, communications that were known to be unrelated to a target, including those that were potentially wholly domestic,[56] could be retained for up to five years so long as the government was not seeking to use that information. The court found that this had the effect of maximizing the retention of such information, and was not consistent with FISA's mandate to minimize the retention of U.S. person information.[57]

The FISC also held that the proposed minimization procedures did not satisfy the Fourth Amendment. In 2008, the Foreign Intelligence Surveillance Court of Review (FISCR) upheld collection activities under the Protect America Act (PAA)[58] that appear to have closely resembled the authority under Section 702.[59] The FISCR first determined that the purposes of foreign intelligence investigations were sufficiently important and different from traditional law enforcement to justify an exception to the warrant requirement. The court went on to hold that surveillance under the PAA was also reasonable since the targeting and minimization procedures used by the government provided sufficient proxies for the traditional particularity and probable cause requirements of the Fourth Amendment. The court especially noted that such procedures were reasonable especially when balanced against the government's interest in protecting national security, which was "of the highest order of magnitude."[60] In contrast, in the October 2011 opinion, the FISC applied the same analysis, but after having first determined that the minimization procedures were statutorily deficient, found that the balance required under the Fourth Amendment's reasonableness test did not favor the government.

A second opinion declassified by the DNI in August 2013 dealt with the aftermath of the October 2011 opinion. Under Section 702, if the FISC disapproves of the proposed minimization procedures, the government may revise those procedures in order to come into compliance.[61] In this case, the government presented revised minimization procedures to the FISC, and the court approved those procedures on November 30, 2011.[62] The revised minimization procedures required the segregation of those communications most likely to involve unrelated or wholly domestic communications; required special handling and markings for those communications which were not segregated to warn analysts; and reduced the retention period from five years to two.[63]

WHAT OVERSIGHT MECHANISMS ARE IN PLACE?

The following is a summary of the oversight mechanisms governing the two intelligence collection programs. Both programs appear to be subject to frequent examination by the FISC, in addition to Congress. However, critics, citing the frequency with which requests are approved by the FISC, argue that the court operates as a "rubber stamp" for the executive branch.[64] Others contend that the FISC is composed of experienced judges and a professional staff and that the frequency of requests approved by the court reflects an iterative, aggressive oversight process. Because of the lack of clarity into the court's decisions, it is difficult to judge the validity of these claims.

Domestic Phone Records: The collection of phone records in bulk is conducted pursuant to FICA orders that, according to intelligence officials, must be renewed every 90 days.[65] The data are then stored at a repository at NSA. The FISC also approves the procedures governing access to those data and has apparently required that NSA meet a *reasonable articulable suspicion standard* prior to searching the data.[66] FISC approval is not necessary prior to searching the data already held at NSA. Rather, 22 individuals at NSA have been authorized to approve requests to query the data and to determine whether information meets the reasonable suspicion standard.[67]

Queries against phone records data are documented and audited by NSA. In 2012, less than 300 phone numbers were used to query the database.[68]

Intelligence officials have identified several additional oversight mechanisms that monitor the implementation of this program. These include (1) a report filed every 30 days with the FISC; (2) a meeting at least every 90 days between the Department of Justice (DOJ), the Office of the Director of National Intelligence (ODNI), and NSA, and (3) a semiannual report to Congress.

Foreign Internet-Related Data: The collection of electronic communications pursuant to Section 702 is subject to a less stringent oversight regime. "[I]nformation is obtained with the FISA Court approval and with the knowledge of the provider based upon a written directive from the Attorney General and the Director of National Intelligence."[69] In accordance with the FISA Amendments Act, procedures governing the program, designed to prevent the acquisition and dissemination of Americans' communications, are subject to court approval.[70] Actual collection of this information does not require a warrant or court order. Decisions regarding whether collection on a foreign target is in keeping with Section 702 appear to take place largely within the DOJ and ODNI.

After data are collected, NSA is subject to a number of oversight reporting procedures. These include (1) quarterly reports to the FISC concerning compliance issues; (2) semi-annual reports to the FISC and Congress that assess compliance with targeting and minimization standards; (3) semi-annual reports to the FISC and Congress on the implementation of the program; and (4) annual reviews from the NSA Inspector General.

ARGUMENTS FOR AND AGAINST THE TWO PROGRAMS

The Administration has argued that the surveillance activities leaked to the press, in addition to being subject to oversight by all three branches of government, are important to national security and have helped disrupt terror plots. These arguments have not always distinguished between the two programs, but generally the Administration appears to have taken the position that collection pursuant to Section 702 is an important tool on a broad range of national security issues and that collection pursuant to Section 215 has been useful in a discrete number of terrorism cases. Regarding bulk phone records, which have come under greater scrutiny, intelligence officials have argued that the breadth of the collection is necessary to ensure all relevant information is available to the government and can be identified through searches in NSA's database, rather than having more focused collection that might miss relevant information. For example, Deputy Attorney General James Cole before the HPSCI stated "if you're looking for a needle in the haystack, you have to get the haystack first."[71]

Intelligence officials initially stated that the two programs have "helped prevent over 50 potential terrorist events"—which appear to encompass both active terror plots targeting the United States homeland and terrorism facilitation activity not tied directly to terrorist attacks at home or abroad.[72] NSA Director General Alexander subsequently clarified these remarks, citing a total of 54 terrorist events. Forty-two of these involved terrorist plots and 12 involved material support to terrorism. Of the total number of terrorist events, 53 somehow involved collection pursuant to Section 702. Thirteen of the 54 involved threats inside the United States, and 12 of those cases somehow utilized the phone records held by NSA.[73]

Intelligence officials have provided one example in which the target of the plot was the U.S. homeland and for which the phone records were somehow utilized. Of the other 11 cases in which the phone records were used, one involved U.S.-based material support for extremist activity outside the United States.[74] It is not clear how many, if any, of the remaining 10 cases that utilized the phone records involved terror plots targeting the U.S. homeland as opposed to U.S.-based material support for terrorism. The Administration has provided four examples:

- **Najibullah Zazi:** NSA, using *702 authorities*, intercepted an email between an extremist in Pakistan and an individual in the United States. NSA provided this email to the FBI, which identified and began to surveil Colorado-based Najibulla Zazi. NSA then received Zazi's phone number from the FBI, checked it against phone records procured using *215 authorities*, and identified one of Zazi's accomplices, an individual named Adis Medunjanin. Zazi and Medunjanin were both subsequently arrested and convicted of planning to bomb the New York City subway.[75] Additional information on this case is offered in the next section.
- **Khalid Ouazzani:** NSA, using *702 authorities*, intercepted communication between an extremist in Yemen and an individual in the United States named Khalid Ouazzani. Ouazzani was later convicted of providing material support to al-Qaeda and admitted to swearing allegiance to the group. The FBI has claimed that Ouazzani

was involved in the early stages of a plot to bomb the New York Stock Exchange.[76]

- **David Headley:** According to intelligence officials, the FBI received information indicating that Headley, a U.S. citizen living in Chicago, was involved in the 2008 attack in Mumbai that took the lives of 160 people. NSA, using *702 authorities*, also became aware of Headley's involvement in a plot to bomb a Danish newspaper. It is unclear from public statements how Headley first came to the FBI's attention. He pled guilty to terrorism charges and admitted to involvement in both the Mumbai attack and Danish newspaper plot.
- **Basaaly Saeed Moalin:** NSA, using phone records pursuant to *215 authorities*, provided the FBI with a phone number for an individual in San Diego who had indirect contacts with extremists overseas. The FBI identified the individual as Basally Saeed Moalin and determined that he was involved in financing extremist activity in Somalia.[77] Moalin was convicted in 2013 of providing material support to al-Shabaab, the Somalia-based al-Qaeda affiliate.[78]

Concerns Regarding Domestic Phone Records: Criticism has increasingly focused on the collection of phone records pursuant to Section 215. The public and Members of Congress have expressed particular concern about data provided to NSA in bulk about U.S. citizens. Critics question the importance of the phone records in the cases identified by the Administration and question whether any value from those records could have been derived from a more traditional court order. Rather than using a phone number to query a database at the NSA, they argue the same number could be given to phone companies to conduct a search of their records. This could produce similar results, although the process of obtaining the order and making a request could take longer. In essence, using the government's needle-in-a-haystack analogy, critics are suggesting that the "haystack" could be utilized to equal effect regardless of whether it is sitting at the NSA or remains in the possession of the phone company. For example, Senators Ron Wyden and Tom Udall, in a statement from June 19, 2013, argued:

> [I]t is still unclear to us why agencies investigating terrorism do not simply obtain this information directly from phone companies using a regular court order. If the NSA is only reviewing those records that meet a "reasonable suspicion" standard, then there is no reason it shouldn't be able to get court orders for the records it actually needs. Making a few hundred of these requests per year would clearly not overwhelm the FISA

> Court. And the law already allows the government to issue emergency authorizations to get these records quickly in urgent circumstances....
>
> [W]e have yet to see any evidence that the bulk phone records collection program has provided any otherwise unobtainable intelligence. It may be more convenient for the NSA to collect this data in bulk, rather than directing specific queries to the various phone companies, but in our judgment convenience alone does not justify the collection of the personal information of huge numbers of ordinary Americans if the same or more information can be obtained using less intrusive methods.[79]

Concerns Regarding Foreign Internet-Related Data: Many critics of Section 702 collection appear to agree that it is a valuable tool for national security, but question whether the program has been implemented, or can be implemented, in a way that adequately protects American civil liberties. Some argue that for certain types of electronic communications, it is not possible to assess with enough confidence whether a prospective target is inside the United States or overseas.

This concern sharpened in August 2013, when the Office of the DNI released the October 2011 FISC opinion in which the court found that some elements of the 702 collection program were inconsistent with the Fourth Amendment of the Constitution. The problem concerned "about" communications and NSA's "upstream collection," which are described earlier in this report. Because of technical constraints, NSA was unable to specifically collect the relevant "about" communication and instead was collecting groupings of communications, which contained communications about legitimate targets as well as communications unrelated to those targets. In some cases, that involved the collection of Americans' communications and of wholly domestic communications. As a result of this overcollection, NSA acquired tens of thousands of domestic communications, which the court determined was in violation of the Constitution.

As discussed above, the FISC allowed the problematic upstream "about" collection to continue but required NSA to implement stricter minimization procedures for tranches of data that might contain Americans' communications. Members may wish to engage intelligence officials about the effectiveness of NSA's "about" communications collection, which does not specifically collect the communications of foreign intelligence targets and might therefore be of less utility than "to/from" communications, which comprise 91% of collection under Section 702. While "about" communications apparently present challenging technical issues, Section 702 might nonetheless be amenable to legislative fixes if the collection that raises the greatest concerns also has the least utility.

Additional Background on Najibullah Zazi

The Zazi case cited by the Administration may help Members evaluate the utility of NSA's bulk phone records collection program. A significant amount of public information about that case has been made available since Zazi's arrest on September 19, 2009. Zazi, Medunjanin, and a third man traveled to Pakistan on August 28, 2008, to receive training from al-Qaeda. Zazi returned to the United States in January 2009.[80] Medunjanin returned in September 2008. On September 6, 2009, Zazi sent an email from Colorado to an associate in Pakistan requesting a recipe for explosives. There is reason to believe this email is the one intercepted by NSA using 702 authorities and then passed to the FBI.[81] The FBI opened an investigation and began surveillance of Zazi on September 7. Zazi traveled from Denver to New York on September 9, 2009, for the purpose of conducting an attack sometime between September 14 to 16. FBI agents observed his departure from Denver. Zazi became aware of FBI surveillance while in New York and chose to return to Denver on September 12. He was interviewed and arrested by the FBI several days later.

It is unclear at what point in the investigation authorities utilized the phone records at NSA to link Zazi to Medunjanin. FBI officials recently acknowledged that they were already aware of Medunjanin, but stated that the information derived from Section 215 collection provided corroborating information regarding Medunjanin's connection to Zazi.[82] At some point in the investigation, the FBI was able to identify travel records showing that Zazi and Medunjanin in 2008 departed for Pakistan together.[83] It has also been reported that the New York Police Department had previously identified both Zazi and Medunjanin using informants and undercover officers at a mosque in Queens.[84] Prospective questions about the role of the phone records in the investigation include the following:

- What did the FBI know about Medunjanin's travel to Pakistan and about his activity more generally prior to linking him with Zazi using the phone records database? Was that information sufficient to link him to Zazi absent a search of those phone records?
- To what extent was the information available to FBI agents in September 2009 sufficient to obtain phone records through a court

order or a National Security Letter, rather than through the repository at NSA?

- Were the phone records connecting Zazi to Medunjanin from before or after their trip to Pakistan in August 2008? In light of when those calls were made, would company retention times for phone records have limited government access to data if those records had been provided pursuant to a more specific court order?
- Was the speed with which authorities were able to access phone records data important to identifying Medunjani or to disrupting the plot? Authorities appear to have had a nine-day window during which they could exploit available information to disrupt the attack. Were phone records utilized within that window?

LEGISLATIVE PROPOSALS

To date, legislative proposals have focused primarily on intelligence collection of domestic phone records. Members of Congress have introduced bills or are circulating draft bills that would limit in various ways the scope of requests for business records that could be covered under Section 215 of the USA PATRIOT ACT of 2001. Answers to the questions above concerning the Zazi case might help elucidate the policy dimensions of these proposals. The Administration has stated that it is currently looking at the architectural framework of the Section 215 collection program and will provide recommendations to Congress on how Section 215 might be changed.[85]

Prospective changes that could require the federal government to make individualized requests to phone companies, rather than requests for phone records in bulk, could also require mandating specific retention times for phone company business records such that those times are consistent with the current five-year period for records held by NSA. The crux of the debate may come down to concerns about the speed with which the government can access phone records that are not held in bulk at NSA. With respect to changes to Section 215, NSA Director General Alexander has stated, "The concern is speed in crisis."[86] The process for identifying prospective terrorists could be slowed to some degree if the government is required to make individual requests rather than having ready access to bulk phone data. One question for Members of Congress may be whether that increased time frame would have been detrimental in any of the roughly 10 cases identified by the intelligence community that involved phone records collected in bulk.

Some Members have also proposed legislation intended to provide greater transparency of opinions of the FISC and FISCR.[87] Under current law, the opinions of either court that include significant construction or interpretation of any provision of FISA must be provided to the judiciary and intelligence committees of the House and the Senate within 45 days.[88] However, the AG and DNI may redact information from those opinions where necessary to protect the national security of the United States and when limited to sensitive sources and methods information or the identities of targets.[89] Recent legislative proposals would further require such opinions to be made public or summarized in an unclassified manner, but would continue to provide discretion for the AG to limit the disclosure of opinions or summaries if necessary to protect national security.

Of the 22 proposals identified below, 16 include changes to Section 215 and 15 of those attempt to limit the bulk collection of phone records by NSA. Eight proposals would change the FISA process by, among other things, requiring greater public disclosure of FISA court decisions or changing the way judges are appointed to the FISA court.

Table 1. Legislative Proposals in the 113th Congress

Proposals	Includes Changes to...			Details
	215	702	FISC	
S. 1182 (Udall)	√			Would amend the business records provision of FISA to require records to pertain to the subject of the investigation, or the subject's activities or acquaintances, in addition to being relevant.
S. 1168 (Sanders, Restore Our Privacy Act)	√			Would amend the business records provision to require "specific and articulable facts" demonstrating that each of the tangible things sought is relevant prior to gaining access to records.
				Expands reporting requirements such that the AG is required to keep Congress fully informed regarding business records requests.

Proposals	Includes Changes to...			Details
	215	702	FISC	
S. 1130 (Merkley, Ending Secret Law Act)	√	√	√	Requires the public disclosure of orders or opinions that include "significant construction or interpretation" of Sections 215 or 702.
H.R. 2475 (Schiff, Ending Secret Law Act)				
H.R. 2440 (Jackson Lee, FISA Court in the Sunshine Act of 2013)				
S. 1121 (Paul, Fourth Amendment Restoration Act of 2013)				Specifies that "The Fourth Amendment to the Constitution shall not be construed to allow any agency of the United States Government to search the phone records of Americans without a warrant based on probable cause."
S. 1215 (Leahy, FISA Accountability and Privacy Protection Act of 2013)	√	√	√	Would, among other things, change the date when Section 702 authorities established in the FISA Amendments Act would expire and limit the scope of requests pursuant to Section 215 in a similar manner as S. 1182.
H.R. 2399 (Conyers, The LIBERT-E Act)	√			Would amend the business records provision to require that records be both relevant and material, as well as pertaining only to the subject of the investigation.
				Requires the AG to make all reports to the Intelligence and Judiciary Committees available to all Members of Congress.
H.Amdt. 413 (Amash)	√			Would have limited the availability of funds for the collection of phone records in bulk.

Table 1. (Continued)

Proposals	Includes Changes to...			Details
	215	702	FISC	
H.Amdt. 412 (Pompeo)	√	√		Would have limited the availability of funds for the targeting of U.S. persons pursuant to Section 702 authorities and for the collection of the content of communications pursuant to Section 215 authorities.
H.R. 2818 (Holt, Surveillance State Repeal Act)	√	√	√	Repeals the USA PATRIOT ACT.
				Repeals the FISA Amendments Act.
				Extends the term limits for FISC judges.
H.R. 2586 (Cohen, FISA Court Accountability Act)			√	Changes how judges are appointed to the FISC such that 8 of 11 judges would be designated by Members of the House and Senate.
H.R. 2761 (Schiff, Presidential Appointment of FISA Court Judges Act)			√	Gives the President the power to appoint, and the Senate the power to confirm, FISC judges.
S. 1467 (Blumenthal, FISA Court Reform ACT of 2013)			√	Establishes a position of Special Advocate with the responsibility to review applications to the FISC and decisions of the court.
				Requires the public disclosure of FISC decisions.
S. 1460 (Blumenthal, FISA Judge Selection Reform Act)			√	Expands the number of FISC judges to 13.
				Changes how judges are appointed to the FISC such that judges are nominated by the chief judge of each judicial circuit and then designated by the Chief Justice of the United States.

Proposals	Includes Changes to...			Details
	215	702	FISC	
H.R. ____ (Fitzpatrick, NSA Accountability Act of 2013)	√			Would amend the business records provision to require that records be both relevant and material, as well as pertaining only to the subject of the investigation.
H.R. 2603 (Ross, Relevancy Act)	√			Would amend the business records provision to require the subject of the investigation to be a specific person or a specific group of persons.
H.R. 2684 (Lynch, Telephone Surveillance Accountability Act of 2013)	√			Would amend the business records provision to prohibit searching telephony metadata, unless a FISA court judge issues an order finding that there is a reasonable, articulable suspicion that the basis of the search is material and specifically relevant to an authorized investigation.
H.R. 2736 (Larsen-Amash, Government Surveillance Transparency Act of 2013)	√	√		Authorizes a private entity that receives an order or directive under FISA to publicly disclose general and aggregate information about the information sought.
H.R. 3035 (Lofgren, Surveillance Order Reporting Act of 2013)	√	√		Permits public reporting by electronic communications providers of estimate of government requests for information.
S. 1452 (Franken, Surveillance Transparency Act of 2013)	√	√		Enhances reports to Congress on number of applications made and orders granted under FISA, as well as estimates on the number of U.S. persons affected.
H.R. 2849 (Lynch, Privacy Advocate General Act of2013)				Establishes an Office of the Privacy Advocate General in the executive branch appointed

Table 1. (Continued)

Proposals	Includes Changes to...			Details
	215	702	FISC	
			√	jointly by Chief Justice and Senior Associate Justice, who would be required to: serve as opposing counsel for FISA applications, and authorized to request disclosure of a FISC order and appeal such orders.

Source: Prepared by CRS.

End Notes

1 U.S. persons are defined in FISA to include U.S. citizens and legal permanent residents, as well as unincorporated associations comprised of a substantial number of U.S. persons and most domestically chartered corporations. 50 U.S.C. §1801(i).

2 Glenn Greenwald, "NSA collecting phone records of millions of Verizon customers daily," *The Guardian*, June 5, 2013.

3 Siobhan Gorman, Even Perez, Janet Hook, "U.S. Collects Vast Data Trove," The Wall Street Journal, June 7, 2013, available at http://online.wsj.com/article/SB10001424127887324299104578529112289298922.html.

4 Ed O'Keefe, "Transcript: Diane Feinstein, Saxby Chambliss explain, defend NSA phone records program," The Washington Post, June 6, 2013, available at http://www.washingtonpost.com/blogs/post-politics/wp/2013/06/06/transcript-dianne-feinstein-saxby-chambliss-explain-defend-nsa-phone-records- program/?print=1.

5 The Office of the Director of National Intelligence, "Director James R. Clapper interview with Andrea Mitchell, NBC News Chief Foreign Affairs Correspondent," June 8, 2013.

6 Metadata generally refers to "data about data" and the term could be used to refer to other information about a phone call that is not currently being collected by the government. See "Understanding Metadata," National Information Standards Organization, 2004, available at http://www.niso.org/publications/press/UnderstandingMetadata.pdf.

7 U.S. Congress, House Permanent Select Committee on Intelligence, *How Disclosed NSA Programs Protect Americans, and Why Disclosure Aids Our Adversaries*, 113th Congress, 1st sess., June 18, 2013.

8 James Clapper, the Office of the Director of National Intelligence, letter to Senator Ron Wyden, July 26, 2013, available at http://www.wyden.senate.gov/news/press-releases/wyden-and-udall-important-surveillance-questions- unanswered

9 *Id.*

10 "Feinstein, Chambliss Statement on NSA Phone Records Program."

11 Glenn Greenwald, Spencer Ackerman, "NSA collected US email records in bulk for more than two years under Obama," *The Guardian*, June 27, 2013, available at http://www.guardian.co.uk/world/2013/jun/27/nsa-data-mining- authorised-obama.

12 House Permanent Select Committee on Intelligence, *How Disclosed NSA Programs Protect Americans, and WhyDisclosure Aids Our Adversaries*.

[13] Office of the Assistant Attorney General, Department of Justice, "Report on the National Security Agency's Bulk Collection Programs Affect by USA PATRIOT Act Reauthorization," December 14, 2009, p. 3, available at http://www.dni.gov/files/documents/2009_CoverLetter_Report_Collection.pdf.

[14] See for example, Representative Nadler's comments in the House Judiciary Committee hearing on FBI oversight, June 13, 2013. "But let me ask you the following: Under Section 215 -- and I -- I would like to associate myself with the remarks that a dragnet subpoena for every - every telephone record, et cetera, every e-mail record, although I know they don't do that anymore, but they could again tomorrow, and they did do it certainly makes a mockery of the relevance of the standard in Section 215. If everything in the world is relevant, then there's no meaning to that word."

[15] Barton Gellman, Laura Poitra, "U.S., British intelligence mining data from nine U.S. Internet companies in broad secret program," *The Washington Post*, June 6, 2013, available at http://articles.washingtonpost.com/2013-06- 06/news/39784046_1_prism-nsa-u-s-servers.

[16] Glenn Greenwald, Ewen MacAskill, "NSA Prism program taps in to user data of Apple, Google and others," *The Guardian*, June 6, 2013, available at http://www.guardian.co.uk/world/2013/jun/06/us-tech-giants-nsa-data.

[17] See for example, Declan McCullagh, "No evidence of NSA's 'direct access' to tech companies," *CNET*, June 7, 2013, available at http://news.cnet.com/8301-13578_3-57588337-38/no-evidence-of-nsas-direct-access-to-tech-companies/.

[18] The Office of the Director of National Intelligence, "DNI Statement on Activities Authorized Under Section 702 of FISA," press release, June 6, 2013.

[19] The Office of the Director of National Intelligence, "DNI Statement on the Collection of Intelligence Pursuant to Section 702 of the Foreign Intelligence Surveillance Act," press release, June 8, 2013.

[20] The President's remarks about the intelligence collection pursuant to 702 referred to "the Internet and emails."

[21] Intelligence officials have stated that communications of a U.S. person that have been inadvertently collected must be promptly destroyed unless they meet specific criteria. Examples cited by the Administration involving individuals inside the United States appear to meet these criteria.

[22] Foreign Intelligence Surveillance Court Memorandum Opinion, Judge John Bates, October 3, 2011, at 29, available at https://www.eff.org/file/37548#page/1/mode/1up.

[23] *Id.*

[24] *Id.*, at 15.

[25] *Id.*, at.17.

[26] The gathering of intelligence information not concerning a U.S. person was authorized by a technical amendment to §215 passed a few months after its enactment. *See* P.L. 107-56, §215, *amended by* P.L. 107-108, §314, *codified at* 50 U.S.C. §1861. Originally subject to sunset on December 31, 2005, §215 has been reauthorized six times since it was originally enacted, and is currently set to expire on June 1, 2015. *See*, P.L. 109-160 (extension until February 3, 2006); P.L. 109-177 (extension until December 31, 2009); P.L. 111-118, §1004 (2009) (extension until February 28, 2010); P.L. 111-141 (extension until February 28, 2011); P.L. 112-3 (extension until May 27, 2011); P.L. 112-14 (extension until June 1, 2015).

[27] Director of National Intelligence James Clapper, *DNI Statement on Recent Unauthorized Disclosures of Classified Information*, June 6, 2013, available at http://www.dni.gov/index.php/newsroom/press-releases/191-press-releases- 2013/868-dni-statement-on-recent-unauthorized-disclosures-of-classified-information. *See also* In re Application of the Federal Bureau of Investigation for an Order Requiring the Production of Tangible Things From [redacted], No. BR 13-80 (For. Intell. Surveillance Ct. Apr. 25, 2013).

[28] Prior to 2001, FISA contained a mechanism for the government to compel the production of certain business records through subpoena-like court orders, but was limited to records from

only four types of businesses: (1) common carriers, (2) public accommodation facilities, (3) storage facilities, and (4) vehicle rental facilities. A court order compelling the production of these records was authorized if the FBI presented the FISC with "specific and articulable facts giving reason to believe that the person to whom the records pertain is a foreign power or an agent of a foreign power." 50 U.S.C. §1862 (2001).

[29] The Supreme Court, in *Smith v. Maryland*, 442 U.S. 735 (1979), has held that there is no Fourth Amendment protected reasonable expectation of privacy in records of telephone calls held in the hands of third party providers, where the content of any call is not intercepted. However, Congress has enacted a number of statutes since the *Smith* decision, such as FISA, that both permit access by the government for foreign intelligence or law enforcement purposes to information relating to telephone numbers dialed from or received by a particular telephone number, as well as duration and usage, while simultaneously imposing limitations as to how such information may be accessed and under what circumstances it may be used.

[30] 50 U.S.C. §1861(b)(2)(A). The statute also considers records presumptively relevant if they pertain to a foreign power or an agent of a foreign power; the activities of a suspected agent of a foreign power who is the subject of such authorized investigation; or an individual in contact with, or known to, a suspected agent of a foreign power who is the subject of such authorized investigation. In 2005, §215 was also amended to provide special protections for records which were considered particularly sensitive. Specifically, if the records sought are "library circulation records, library patron lists, book sales records, book customer lists, firearms sales records, tax return records, educational records, or medical records containing information that would identify a person," the application must be approved by one of three high-ranking FBI officers, and cannot be further delegated. Currently, the three FBI officials who are permitted to approve such an application are Director James B. Comey; Deputy Director Sean M. Joyce; and Executive Assistant Director for National Security Stephanie Douglas. *See* 50 U.S.C. §1861(a)(3) *and* FBI, *About Us: Executives*, available at http://www.fbi.gov/about-us/executives/director.

[31] *See* U.S. v. Banks, 540 U.S. 31, 36 (2003) (forced entry into premises during execution of search warrant is permissible if there are reasonable grounds to expect futility of knocking, or if circumstances support a reasonable suspicion of exigency when the officers arrive at the door). Courts have eschewed using bright line rules to determine whether "reasonable suspicion" is warranted, and have required an examination of the totality of the circumstances instead. *See* U.S. v. Hensley, 469 U.S. 221, 227 (1985) (an informant's detailed statements implicating a third party in a bank robbery were sufficient to provide the reasonable suspicion necessary to justify a law enforcement stop of that third party); U.S. v. Brignoni-Ponce, 422 U.S. 873, 881–82, (1975) (the simple fact that a vehicle's occupants appear to be of Mexican ancestry is insufficient to provide law enforcement officers with reasonable grounds to believe that those individuals are aliens); Terry v. Ohio, 392 U.S. 1 (1968) (police officer's observation of individual repeatedly walking back and forth in front of storefronts and peering inside store windows provided reasonable suspicion that individuals were armed and about to engage in criminal activity justifying stop and frisk).

[32] 18 U.S.C. §2703(d). Note that the SCA also requires that the information be "material" rather than just "relevant."

[33] U.S. v. Warshak, 631 F.3d 266 (6th Cir. 2010).

[34] An IP address is a numerical designation for a particular computer or device on a network that is used to facilitate routing of communications to and from that computer or device.

[35] U.S. v. Perrine, 518 F.3d 1196 (10th Cir. 2008).

[36] *See* Fed. R. Evid. §401 ("Evidence is relevant if ... it has any tendency to make a fact more or less probable than it would be without the evidence ..."); *and* Black's Law Dictionary (7th ed.) (defining relevant as "logically connected and tending to prove or disprove a matter in issue; having appreciable or probative value – that is, rationally tending to persuade people of the probability or possibility of some alleged fact.").

[37] Obama Administration Whitepaper, *Bulk Collection of Telephony Metadata under Section 215 of the USA PATRIOT ACT*, Aug. 9, 2013, available at https://www.eff.org/document/administration-white-paper-section-215-patriot-act.

[38] Oppenheimer Fund, Inc. v. Sanders, 437 U.S. 340, 351 (1978).

[39] Whitepaper at 10 (citing Carrillo Huettel, LLP v. SEC, 2011 WL 601369 (S.D. Cal. Feb. 11, 2011); Goshawk Dedicated Ltd. v. Am. Viatical Servs., LLC, 2007 WL 3492762 (N.D. Ga. Nov. 5, 2007); and Chen-Oster v. Goldman, Sachs & Co., 285 F.R.D. 294 (S.D.N.Y. 2012)).

[40] *E.g.* in *Carrillo Huettel*, the court upheld the subpoena notwithstanding the possibility that the database would include account information for only hundreds of customers.

[41] 50 U.S.C. §1861(a)(2).

[42] Attorney General's Guidelines for Domestic FBI Operations (Sept. 29, 2008), available at http://www.justice.gov/ag/readingroom/guidelines.pdf. *See also* CRS Report R41780, *The Federal Bureau of Investigation and Terrorism Investigations*, by Jerome P. Bjelopera.

[43] Director of National Intelligence James Clapper, *Facts on the Collection of Intelligence Pursuant to Section 702 of the Foreign Intelligence Surveillance Act*, June 8, 2013, available at http://www.dni.gov/index.php/newsroom/press- releases/191-press-releases-2013/871-facts-on-the-collection-of-intelligence-pursuant-to-section-702-of-the-foreign-intelligence-surveillance-act.

[44] 50 U.S.C. §1805(a)(3) (2008) (electronic surveillance); *Id.* at §1824(a)(3) (physical searches). In contrast, federal criminal search warrants require probable cause to believe that instrumentalities, evidence, or fruits of a crime will be found in the place to be searched. *See* Fed. R. Crim. P. 41(c). Criminal warrants authorizing electronic surveillance additionally require probable cause to believe that the target is engaged in criminal activities, that normal investigative techniques are insufficient, and that the facilities that are the subject of surveillance will be used by the target. 18 U.S.C. §2518(3) (2008).

[45] 50 U.S.C. §1881a(b).

[46] 50 U.S.C. §1881a(g)(2)(A)(vi).

[47] The certification must also attest that guidelines have been adopted to ensure that the specifically prohibited types of surveillance activities listed in §702(b), such as reverse targeting, are not conducted.

[48] U.S. Const. amend. IV.

[49] *See* Katz v. United States, 389 U.S. 347, 357 (1967) ("[S]earches conducted outside the judicial process without prior approval by judge or magistrate are per se unreasonable under the Fourth Amendment—subject only to a few specifically established and well delineated exceptions.").

[50] Also called the "general balancing," "general reasonableness," or "totality-of-the circumstances" test, it requires a court to determine the constitutionality of a search or seizure "by assessing, on the one hand, the degree to which [a search or seizure] intrudes upon an individual's privacy and, on the other, the degree to which it is needed for the promotion of legitimate governmental interests." Samson v. California, 547 U.S. 843, 848 (2006).

[51] U.S. v. U.S. District Court, 407 U.S. 297, 321-24 (1972) (also referred to as the *Keith* case, so named for the District Court judge who initially ordered disclosure of unlawful warrantless electronic surveillance to the defendants).

[52] *Id.* at 321-22. *See also* In re Directives Pursuant to Section 105b of the Foreign Intelligence Surveillance Act, 551 F.3d 1004 (U.S. Foreign Intell. Survellance Ct. Rev. 2008) (holding that the foreign intelligence surveillance of targets reasonably believed to be outside of the U.S. qualifies for the "special needs" exception to the warrant requirement).

[53] *See* Office of the DNI, *DNI Declassifies Intelligence Community Documents Regarding Collection Under Section 702 of the Foreign Intelligence Surveillance Act (FISA)*, Aug. 21, 2013, available at http://icontherecord.tumblr.com/post/58944252298/dni-declassifies-intelligence-community-documents.

[54] Foreign Intelligence Surveillance Court Memorandum Opinion, at 59-63, 67-80 (Oct. 3, 2011).

[55] *Id*, at 67-79 (Oct. 3, 2011). The FISC upheld the targeting provisions, even though the government acknowledged that its upstream collection activities were known to acquire some wholly domestic communications. The FISC found that this was not a violation of Section 702, since the government could not determine "at the time of acquisition" whether a particular communication was wholly domestic. Foreign Intelligence Surveillance Court Memorandum Opinion, at 46-47 (Oct. 3, 2011).

[56] If a communication is recognized as being wholly domestic, it would have been purged from the system under the proposed minimization procedures.

[57] *Id.* at 59.

[58] P.L. 110-55. The Protect America Act expired after approximately six months, on February 16, 2008.

[59] In re Directives Pursuant to Section 105b of the Foreign Intelligence Surveillance Act, 551 F.3d 1004, 1009-1016 (U.S. Foreign Intell. Surveil Ct. Rev. 2008) (upholding similar joint authorization procedure under the Protect America Act in the face of a Fourth Amendment challenge brought by telecommunications provider).

[60] *Id.* at 1012.

[61] 50 U.S.C. §1881a(i)(3)(B).

[62] Foreign Intelligence Surveillance Court Memorandum Opinion, at 11-15 (Nov. 30, 2011).

[63] *Id.* at 7-11. A third and final declassified order was issued in September of 2012 and addressed the question of what to do with the information that had been acquired through upstream collection prior to the October 2011 opinion. In this third opinion, the FISC acknowledged that the NSA had made a "corporate decision" to purge all data identified as originating from upstream collection before October 31, 2011 (the date that the revised minimization procedures went into effect). Foreign Intelligence Surveillance Court Memorandum Opinion, at 11-15 (Sept. 2012).

[64] For example, from 2010 to 2012, the court granted all but one of the government's 5,180 requests. See "Foreign Intelligence Surveillance Act Court Orders 1979-2011," The Electronic Privacy Information Center, available at http://epic.org/privacy/wiretap/stats/fisa_stats.html

[65] House Permanent Select Committee on Intelligence, *How Disclosed NSA Programs Protect Americans, and Why Disclosure Aids Our Adversaries.*

[66] For a discussion of the "reasonable articulable suspicion" standard, *see supra* note 19 and accompanying text.

[67] House Permanent Select Committee on Intelligence, How Disclosed NSA Programs Protect Americans, and Why Disclosure Aids Our Adversaries.

[68] *Id.*

[69] The Office of the Director of National Intelligence, "Facts on the Collection of Intelligence Pursuant to Section 702 of the Foreign Intelligence Surveillance Act," press release, June 8, 2013.

[70] P.L. 110-261.

[71] House Permanent Select Committee on Intelligence, *How Disclosed NSA Programs Protect Americans, and Why Disclosure Aids Our Adversaries.*

[72] *Id.*

[73] General Keith Alexander, "Clear and Present Danger: Cyber-Crime; Cyber-Espionage; Cyber-Terror; and Cyber- War," comments before the Aspen Security Forum, July 18, 2013, available at http://aspensecurityforum.org/2013-video.

[74] *Id.*

[75] Intelligence community backgrounder on NSA surveillance, available at http://www.fas.org/sgp/news/2013/06/ic- back.pdf.

[76] Brian Ross, Aaron Katersky, James Gordon, and Lee Ferran, "NSA Claim of Thwarted NYSE Plot Contradicted by Court Documents," *ABC News*, June 19, 2013, available at http://

abcnews.go.com/Blotter/nsa-claim-thwarted-nyse-plot-contradicted-court-documents/story?id=19436557.

[77] Peter Bergen, David Sterman, "What U.S. learned from listening in on terror group calls," CNN, June 19, 2013.

[78] The Federal Bureau of Investigation, "San Diego Jury Convicts Four Somali Immigrants of Providing Support to Foreign Terrorists," press release, February 22, 2013, available at http://www.fbi.gov/sandiego/press-releases/2013/san-diego-jury-convicts-four-somali-immigrants-of-providing-support-to-foreign-terrorists.

[79] "Wyden, Udall Issue Statement on Effectiveness of Declassified NSA Programs," press release, June 19, 2013, available at http://www.wyden.senate.gov/news/press-releases/wyden-udall-issue-statement-on-effectiveness-of- declassified-nsa-programs.

[80] Transcript of Record, U.S. v. Zazi, No. 1:10-CR-60 (E.D.N.Y. July 18, 2011).

[81] Intelligence officials have stated that an email collected using 702 authorities provided the key lead in the Zazi case. Separately, FBI officials in 2011 stated that they were tipped off to Zazi's activity when they were provided with his email from September 6th, 2009, to associates in Pakistan.

[82] U.S. Congress, House Judiciary Committee, *Oversight of the Foreign Intelligence Surveillance Act Authorities,* 113th Congress, 1st sess., July 17, 2013.

[83] Transcript of Record, U.S. v. Zazi, No. 1:10-CR-60 (E.D.N.Y. July 18, 2011).

[84] Adam Goldman, Eileen Sullivan, Matt Apuzzo, "NYPD's spying programs produced mixed results," December 23, 2011, available at http://abclocal.go.com/kfsn/story?section=news/national_world&id=8477480.

[85] House Permanent Select Committee on Intelligence, *How Disclosed NSA Programs Protect Americans, and Why Disclosure Aids Our Adversaries.*

[86] *Id.*

[87] The precise boundaries of Congress's authority to require the declassification of material classified by the executive have not been fully explored. In one of the few cases to address disputes between the legislative and executive branches over access to classified information, the D.C. Circuit rejected the argument that the executive branch exercises plenary and exclusive authority over access to national security information. U.S. v. AT&T, 551 F.2d 384 (D.C. Cir. 1976). However, in practice, disputes of this matter are typically resolved through voluntary, mutually agreeable accommodation by the branches, rather than resort to judicial enforcement of asserted legal rights.

[88] 50 U.S.C. §1871(c)(1). Any judge who authors an opinion, order, or other decision may request that it be published. If the presiding judge chooses to direct publication of that order, the court may have the executive review and redact it as necessary. Foreign Intel. Surveillance Ct. R. 62.

[89] 50 U.S.C. §1871(d).

In: NSA Intelligence Collection, Leaks ... ISBN: 978-1-62948-937-7
Editor: Simon Cepeda

Chapter 2

SECURITY CLEARANCE PROCESS: ANSWERS TO FREQUENTLY ASKED QUESTIONS*

Michelle D. Christensen and Frederick M. Kaiser

SUMMARY

This report provides a primer on some of the fundamental aspects of the security clearance process, using a "Frequently Asked Questions" format.

A security clearance is a determination that an individual—whether a direct federal employee or a private contractor performing work for the government—is eligible for access to classified national security information. A security clearance alone does not grant an individual access to classified materials. Rather, a security clearance means that an individual is eligible for access. In order to gain access to specific classified materials, an individual should also have a demonstrated "need to know" the information contained in the specific classified materials.

There are three levels of security clearances: Confidential, Secret, and Top Secret, which correspond to the levels of sensitivity of the information that a cleared individual will be eligible to access. In addition, there are two major categories of classified information that are commonly associated with the Top Secret level: Sensitive Compartmented Information (SCI), which refers to intelligence sources and methods, and Special Access Programs (SAPs), which

* This is an edited, reformatted and augmented version of a Congressional Research Service Publication, CRS Report for Congress R43216, dated September 9, 2013.

refers to highly sensitive policies, projects, and programs. These categories exist for classified information that has been deemed particularly vulnerable. Eligibility standards and investigative requirements for access to SCI and SAPs are higher than for access to information otherwise classified at the same level, which further restricts the number of individuals eligible for access.

Federal employees and private contractors must be cleared in order to gain access to classified materials. An individual may not obtain or initiate a security clearance on his or her own. A sponsoring federal agency initiates the process and will make the final security clearance determination based on a background investigation.

Although the process involves a number of stages, four key steps to obtaining and maintaining a security clearance are (1) agency sponsorship and submission of clearance application materials; (2) a background investigation, the extent of which may vary by level of clearance; (3) an adjudication to determine whether an individual will be deemed eligible for access; and (4) periodic reinvestigations. Adjudication and final clearance determinations are generally made by the sponsoring agency. To maintain a security clearance, an individual is also subject to periodic reinvestigations. The frequency of reinvestigations vary by level of clearance.

The Office of Personnel Management, Federal Investigative Services (OPM-FIS) oversees approximately 90% of all background investigations. Typically, the costs of a background investigation, including background investigations of private contractors, are paid for by the requesting agency. While the final determination to grant or deny a security clearance is typically made by the requesting agency, with certain exceptions a security clearance granted by one agency may be accepted by other agencies. It is difficult, however, to determine the degree to which reciprocity occurs between agencies.

INTRODUCTION

The security clearance process is designed to determine the trustworthiness of an individual prior to granting him or her access to classified national security information. The process has evolved since the early 1950s, with antecedents dating to World War II.[1] This report highlights some of the fundamental aspects of the process by providing answers to frequently asked questions.[2]

WHAT IS A SECURITY CLEARANCE?

A security clearance[3] is a determination that an individual—whether a direct federal employee or a private contractor—is eligible for access to classified national security information.[4] A security clearance may only be granted by a federal agency, and generally only upon completion of a background investigation.[5] Using information obtained during the background investigation, the agency will make a determination as to the character and trustworthiness of the individual, and decide if he or she will be eligible for access to classified national security information.

A security clearance alone does not grant an individual access to specific classified materials. Rather, a security clearance means that an individual is eligible for access. In order to gain access to specific classified materials, an individual should also have a demonstrated "need to know" the classified information for his or her position and policy area responsibilities. In addition, prior to accessing classified information, an individual must sign an appropriate nondisclosure agreement.[6]

WHAT IS THE DIFFERENCE BETWEEN A SECURITY CLEARANCE AND A SUITABILITY CHECK?

A security clearance, as noted above, is designed to determine eligibility for access to classified information. A suitability check, which may involve many of the same investigative elements as a security clearance investigation, is designed to authorize employment by the federal government. Unlike a security clearance, a suitability determination does not convey access to classified information.[7]

WHAT ARE THE LEVELS OF SECURITY CLEARANCES?

The levels of security clearances correspond to the levels of sensitivity of the information that cleared individuals will be eligible to access.[8] The three levels, in ascending order, are

- Confidential, the unauthorized disclosure of which would "cause damage to the national security";

- Secret, the unauthorized disclosure of which would "cause serious damage to the national security"; and
- Top Secret, the unauthorized disclosure of which would "cause exceptionally grave damage to the national security."[9]

In addition, there are two major categories of classified information that are commonly associated with the Top Secret level: Sensitive Compartmented Information (SCI), which refers to intelligence sources and methods, and Special Access Programs (SAPs), which refers to highly sensitive policies, projects, and programs.[10] These categories exist for classified information that has been deemed particularly vulnerable. Eligibility standards and investigative requirements for access to SCI and SAPs are higher than for other information classified at the same level, which further restricts the number of individuals that are eligible for access.[11]

WHO IS ELIGIBLE TO OBTAIN A SECURITY CLEARANCE?

An individual who is performing work for the federal government—whether that individual is a direct government employee or a private contractor—may be eligible to obtain a security clearance if his or her work requires access to classified materials. With certain limited exceptions,[12] an individual must hold a security clearance in order to gain access to classified materials.

Generally, only U.S. citizens are eligible to obtain a security clearance.[13] Under Executive Order 12968, with limited exceptions,

> eligibility for access to classified information shall be granted only to employees who are United States citizens for whom an appropriate investigation has been completed and whose personal and professional history affirmatively indicates loyalty to the United States, strength of character, trustworthiness, honesty, reliability, discretion, and sound judgment, as well as freedom from conflicting allegiances and potential for coercion, and willingness and ability to abide by regulations governing the use, handling, and protection of classified information.[14]

CAN AN INDIVIDUAL OBTAIN A SECURITY CLEARANCE ON HIS OR HER OWN?

An individual may not obtain or initiate a security clearance on his or her own. An individual seeking employment with the federal government, or who wishes to do work as a contractor for the government, may be interested in obtaining a security clearance on his or her own, believing that holding a security clearance may expedite the hiring process, or provide him or her with an advantage when competing for government contracts. Yet, only a sponsoring agency may initiate the security clearance process.[15]

According to the Office of Personnel Management (OPM), "clearances are based on investigations requested by Federal agencies, appropriate to specific positions and their duties. Until a person is offered such a position, the government will not request or pay for an investigation for a clearance."[16]

ARE CONSTITUTIONAL OFFICERS (E.G., THE PRESIDENT, MEMBERS OF CONGRESS) REQUIRED TO HOLD A SECURITY CLEARANCE TO ACCESS CLASSIFIED INFORMATION?

Security clearances are not mandated for the President, Vice President, Members of Congress, Supreme Court Justices, or other constitutional officers. The criteria for election or appointment to these positions are specified in the U.S. Constitution, and except by constitutional amendment, no additional criteria (e.g., holding a security clearance) may be required.[17]

As Commander-in-Chief, the President has the authority to establish the standards for access to classified national security information. This authority is typically exercised through the issuance of executive orders. Executive Order 13467, which covers suitability checks and security clearances for federal employees, applicants, and contractors, includes a determination of which executive branch individuals are covered and which are exempted.

> 'Covered individual' means a person who performs work for or on behalf of the executive branch, or who seeks to perform work for or on behalf of the executive branch, but does not include:

(i) the President or (except to the extent otherwise directed by the President) employees of the President under section 105 or 107 of title 3, United States Code; or

(ii) the Vice President or (except to the extent otherwise directed by the Vice President) employees of the Vice President under section 106 of title 3 or annual legislative branch appropriations acts.[18]

Are Congressional Staff and Judicial Staff Required to Hold a Security Clearance to Gain Access to Classified Information?

Congressional staff and judicial staff are required to hold security clearances to gain access to classified information. The requirements are established, for the most part, by public laws, congressional rules, and judicial procedures.

For example, the *Rules of Procedure* of the U.S. Foreign Intelligence Surveillance Court states that "each member of the Court's staff must possess security clearances at a level commensurate to the individual's responsibilities."[19] Within Congress, the Office of House Security and the Office of Senate Security require staff that need access to classified information to have security clearances and to sign nondisclosure agreements in order to be eligible for access to classified national security information.[20]

How Many Individuals Hold Security Clearances in Total and at Each Level?

According to the Office of the Director of National Intelligence (ODNI), approximately 4.9 million individuals held security clearances (of any level) as of October 1, 2012. This includes 3,507,782 security clearances at the Confidential or Secret level and 1,409,969 security clearances at the Top Secret level.[21]

A total of 798,618 security clearance adjudications were approved during FY2012.[22] This includes 511,476 clearances approved at the Confidential or Secret level and 287,142 at the Top Secret level.[23] It is important to note that the number of security clearances approved in FY2012 includes initial clearances and renewals of existing clearances that were subject to reinvestigation in FY2012. For this reason, the number of clearances approved does not reflect the number of new clearances issued.

Table 1 provides a breakdown of these figures by government and contractor employees.

WHAT ARE THE MAJOR ASPECTS OF THE SECURITY CLEARANCE PROCESS?

Although the security clearance process involves a number of stages, the key steps to obtaining and maintaining a security clearance are pre-investigation, investigation, adjudication, and reinvestigation.

- **Pre-Investigation.** During this phase, the agency makes a determination that an employee or contractor requires access to classified information for the completion of his or her duties. At the request of the sponsoring agency, the individual will submit his or her clearance application material (e.g., Standard Form SF86).
- **Investigation.** Using the information provided by the applicant in his or her clearance application materials, a background investigation of the applicant is conducted. OPM oversees over 90% of background investigations.[24] The background investigation may vary in terms of content, cost, and length of time for completion depending, in part, on the level of clearance being sought.[25]
- **Adjudication.** Once the background investigation is complete, the application enters the adjudication phase. During this phase, a determination is made whether to grant the applicant a security clearance. Generally, this decision is made by the sponsoring agency and is based on the information obtained during the background investigation.
- **Reinvestigation.** Individuals who hold security clearances are subject to periodic reinvestigations. The frequency of reinvestigations may vary across agencies, though they are typically conducted at regular intervals depending on the level of clearance. A reinvestigation for someone with a Confidential clearance, the least demanding, is at least once every 15 years from the closing date of the previous investigation; Secret, at least once every 10 years; and Top Secret, at least once every 5 years.[26]

Table 1. Security Clearances Approved and Total Clearances Held as of FY2012

	Government Employees		Contractor/Other Employees	
	Approved in FY2012	Total as of End of FY2012	Approved in FY2012	Total as of End of FY2012
Confidential/Secret	364, 498	2,757,333	146,978	750,449
Top Secret	140,016	791,200	147,126	618,769
Total	504,514	3,548,533	294,104	1,369,218

Source: Office of the Director of National Intelligence, *2012 Report on Security Clearance Determinations*, pp. 3-4.

Notes: Contractor/Other Employees includes figures reported for contractor employees and individuals who could not be identified as either government employees or contractor employees. The ODNI report consolidates the data on Confidential and Secret level security clearance determinations.

ARE PRIVATE CONTRACTORS SUBJECT TO THE SAME CLEARANCE PROCESS AS DIRECT GOVERNMENT EMPLOYEES?

Private contractors are subject to the same clearance procedures as direct government employees. As noted above, an individual may not obtain or initiate a security clearance on his or her own. The process to obtain a security clearance must be initiated by a sponsoring federal agency. The process differs slightly for an individual who is employed by a company that performs work under contract with the federal government. First, the contractor must determine whether the employee requires access to classified information in order to perform the duties of his or her position.[27] The contractor must inform the sponsoring agency (i.e., the "customer" agency for whom the work is being performed) that the employee requires access to classified materials. The sponsoring agency will consider the request and then determine whether to initiate the security clearance process for the employee.[28]

Which Agencies Are Responsible for Conducting Background Investigations?

The Office of Personnel Management, Federal Investigative Services (OPM-FIS) oversees approximately 90% of all background investigations.[29] The actual investigations, for the most part, are conducted by private investigative firms under contract with OPM-FIS. According to Merton W. Miller, Associate Director of Investigations for OPM-FIS, the nationwide network of OPM-FIS investigators includes more than 2,500 federal employees and 6,700 contractors.[30] Of the investigative work conducted by contractors, approximately 45% is conducted by US Investigations Services, LLC (USIS).[31] Most of the remaining investigative work by contractors is conducted by three companies: CACI Premier Technology (CACI), Omniplex World Services Corporation (OMNI), and KeyPoint Government Solutions (KeyPoint).[32]

In certain instances, an agency may have jurisdiction to conduct all or some of its own security clearance background investigations. For example, the Federal Bureau of Investigation (FBI), the U.S. Marshals Service (USMS), and the Bureau of Alcohol, Tobacco, Firearms, and Explosives (ATF) have authority to conduct security clearance background investigations of certain categories of contractor positions.[33] The Central Intelligence Agency (CIA) has authority to conduct its own security clearance background investigations.[34] The CIA also conducts background investigations for ODNI employees and contractors.[35]

Who Pays for Background Investigations?

Typically, the requesting agency pays for background investigations of federal employees and contractor employees.[36] As stated above, the vast majority of federal background investigations (over 90%) are handled by OPM-FIS, which charges other federal agencies for the investigations it oversees.[37] The cost of background investigations vary depending on the level of clearance requested and the scope of the investigation conducted.[38]

The requesting agency is also responsible for any costs associated with the adjudication process and period reinvestigations. The requesting agency is also responsible for certain costs arising from an applicant's appeal of a security clearance denial or revocation, or an applicant's challenge of certain aspects of his or her background investigation (e.g., an appeal of unfavorable results of a polygraph examination).[39]

On Average, How Long Does it Take to Obtain a Security Clearance?

The ODNI's *2012 Report on Security Clearance Determinations* provides data on the longest and shortest security clearance processing times for each element of the intelligence community.[40] For FY2012, the longest processing time for the fastest 90% of Top Secret security clearance cases— from initiation to adjudication decision—ranged from 73 days for the Department of State to 454 days for the CIA. For Secret or Confidential Clearances, the longest processing time for the fastest 90% ranged from 56 days for the Department of State to 500 days for the CIA.

The ODNI's *IRTPA Title III Annual Report for 2010* provides average processing times, and notes that "overall, the government has continued to show a significant improvement in security clearance processing times, reducing the combined investigative and adjudicative processing time from an average of 165 days in 2006 to an average of 53 days in the 4th [quarter of] FY 2010 for the fastest 90% of initial security clearances government-wide."[41]

Are There Guidelines or Standards for Approving, Denying, or Revoking a Security Clearance?

There are 13 adjudicative guidelines that government agencies must use when making security clearance determinations.[42] The guidelines are explained in Title 32 of the *U.S. Code of Federal Regulation*, and cover (1) allegiance to the United States; (2) foreign influence; (3) foreign preference; (4) sexual behavior; (5) personal conduct; (6) financial considerations; (7) alcohol consumption; (8) drug involvement; (9) emotional, mental, and personality disorders; (10) criminal conduct; (11) security violations; (12) outside activities; and (13) misuse of information technology systems.[43]

Each guideline describes the associated circumstances that could raise a security concern and notes which circumstances may be disqualifying. Adverse information regarding one of the guidelines will not automatically result in denial of a security clearance.[44] Adjudicators are instructed to consider the recentness of the information and whether it demonstrates a recurring pattern of adverse behavior.[45] Adjudicators are also instructed to consider any conditions that could mitigate the associated security concerns.[46]

CAN THE OUTCOME OF A SECURITY CLEARANCE DETERMINATION BE APPEALED?

An individual who applied for a clearance may appeal an unfavorable outcome of the determination. Each agency that is responsible for adjudicating and granting security clearances has its own policies and procedures governing the appeal of a security clearance determination.[47] In addition, some agencies may allow applicants to appeal or challenge unfavorable results of a polygraph examination that was conducted as part of his or her security clearance background investigation.[48] Appeals are typically handled within the agency and decided by the agency's personal security appeals board or by an administrative judge.[49] While the outcome of a security clearance determination may be appealed, security clearance decisions are generally not subject to judicial review.[50]

MAY A SECURITY CLEARANCE GRANTED BY ONE AGENCY BE ACCEPTED BY OTHER AGENCIES?

With certain exceptions, a security clearance granted by one agency must be accepted by other agencies, though it is difficult to determine the degree to which reciprocity of security clearance background investigations and determinations actually occurs between agencies. Under Section 3001(d) of the Intelligence Reform and Terrorism Prevention Act (IRTPA) of 2004, "all security clearance background investigations and determinations completed by an authorized investigative agency or authorized adjudication agency shall be accepted by all agencies."[51] There are, however, exceptions to this general principle, particularly among Top Secret, SCI, and SAPs. For example, each agency has authority to conduct an additional investigation if the one on record is a certain number of years old, and each agency may add additional requirements to the process, such as a polygraph examination. Reports by the Government Accountability Office (GAO) and ODNI cite anecdotal evidence which suggests that agencies may be reluctant to accept the background investigations or security clearance determinations made by other agencies.[52]

End Notes

[1] Executive Order 10450, "Security Requirements for Government Employment," 18 *Federal Register* 2489, was issued by President Eisenhower on April 27, 1953. E.O. 10450 established that "the appointment of each civilian officer or employee in any department or agency of the government shall be made subject to investigation." While E.O. 10450 has been amended by subsequent executive orders, it has never been revoked and remains in effect.

[2] Generally, this report will speak about the security clearance process broadly. Where appropriate, any differences in the process that result from variances in the levels of security clearance will be noted. For example, the background investigation (and associated cost) will vary based on the level of security clearance being sought. These differences are discussed later in the report, under the sections titled "What Are the Major Aspects of the Security Clearance Process?" and "Who Pays for Background Investigations?"

[3] The term *security clearance* is not defined in statute. This definition is derived from executive orders, statutes, and directives where the term *security clearance* is used but not defined.

[4] The government also issues security clearances to non-government facilities, such as university laboratories or commercial production facilities, within which contract work for the government is performed. The procedures and policies for granting facility clearances are outside the scope of this report. It is important to note, however, that each individual who performs work within a cleared facility must hold a security clearance if the work requires access to classified information. For information about the facility clearance process, see the Department of Defense (DOD), Defense Security Service's publications "Checklist for a New Facility Clearance" and "Facility Clearance Process FAQs," at http://www.dss.mil/isp/fac_clear/fac_clear.html.

[5] For additional information on background investigations, see the section of this report titled "What Are the Major Aspects of the Security Clearance Process?"

[6] For example, see Standard Form 312, "Classified Information Nondisclosure Agreement," at http://www.gsa.gov/ portal/forms/download/116218.

[7] 5 C.F.R. § 731.202 contains the criteria for making suitability determinations.

[8] The level at which a specific piece of information is classified (i.e., Confidential, Secret, or Top Secret) is determined by the agency or agencies that maintain "ownership" of the information. While guidelines exist for determining the level at which certain information should be classified, there may be dissimilarities in the types of information that different agencies classify at each level. Consequently, there may be differences in the types of positions that each agency would categorize as requiring a "Confidential," "Secret," or "Top Secret" level clearance.

[9] Executive Order 13526, "Classified National Security Information," 75 *Federal Register* 707, December 29, 2009.

[10] Generally, SCI and SAPs are associated with the "Top Secret" clearance level, though DOD regulations suggest that at least some SAPs may be classified at the "Secret" level. See Department of Defense, *National Industrial Security Program Operating Manual*, DOD 5220.22-M, March 28, 2013, p. C-4, at http://www.dtic.mil/whs/directives/corres/pdf/522022m.pdf. Also see U.S. Army, *Special Access Programs (SAPs) and Sensitive Activities*, Army Regulation 380-381, April 21, 2004, at http://www.apd.army.mil/jw2/xmldemo/r380_381/head.asp.

[11] Individuals seeking access to SCI or SAPs are typically subject to additional clearance procedures. See Executive Order 12958, "Classified National Security Information," as amended, 60 *Federal Register* 19825, April 17, 1995; and Office of the Director of National Intelligence, *Personnel Security Standards and Procedures Governing Eligibility for Access to Sensitive Compartmented Information and Other Controlled Access Program Information*, October 1, 2008, at http://www.dni.gov/files/documents/ICD/ICD_704.pdf.

[12] See the section of this report titled "Are Constitutional Officers (e.g., the President, Members of Congress) Required to Hold a Security Clearance to Access Classified Information?"

[13] Under "compelling" circumstances, an agency may grant limited access to non-U.S. citizens who possess a special expertise and "only if the prior 10 years of the subject's life can be appropriately investigated." Executive Order 12968, "Access to Classified Information," 60 *Federal Register* 40245, August 2, 1995.

[14] Ibid. Under "exceptional circumstances" an individual may be granted temporary access to classified information prior to the completion of an investigation.

[15] A sponsoring agency may, however, initiate the security clearance background investigation process for a new government employee prior to his or her start date. Generally, the background investigation for a new government employee begins after the agency extends a tentative offer of employment to the selectee. Office of Personnel Management, *Hiring Elements End-to-End Hiring Roadmap*, 2011, p. 8, http://www.opm.gov/policy-data-oversight/ human-capital-management/hiring-reform/hiringelements.pdf.

[16] See http://www.opm.gov/investigations/background-investigations/.

[17] For example, qualifications for Members of Congress may be found in Article I, Section 2, clause 2, of the U.S. Constitution, and qualifications for President may be found in Article II, Section 1, clause 5. Also see *Powell v. McCormack*, 395 U.S. 486 (1969).

[18] Executive Order 13467, "Reforming Processes Relating to Suitability for Government Employment, Fitness for Contractor Employees, and Eligibility for Access to Classified National Security Information," 73 *Federal Register* 38103, July 2, 2008. The statutory provisions cited in the order refer to sections of law that provide for the appointment of certain personnel within the Executive Office of the President.

[19] Foreign Intelligence Surveillance Court, "Title II: National Security Information," in *Rules of Procedure*, November 1, 2010, p. 1, at http://www.uscourts.gov/uscourts/rules/FISC2010.pdf.

[20] U.S. Senate, Office of Senate Security (OSS), *Security Manual* (revised, 2007), p. 8. Also see CRS Report RS20748, *Protection of Classified Information by Congress: Practices and Proposals*, by Frederick M. Kaiser.

[21] Office of the Director of National Intelligence, *2012 Report on Security Clearance Determinations*, January 2013, p. 3, at http://www.dni.gov/index.php/newsroom/reports-and-publications/193-reports-publications-2013/841-2012- report-on-security-clearance-determinations. The ODNI report consolidates the data on Confidential and Secret level security clearance determinations, and does not provide separate figures for the two levels.

[22] Ibid., p. 4.

[23] Ibid.

[24] For additional information, see the section of this report titled "Which Agencies Are Responsible for Conducting Background Investigations?"

[25] For example, some but not all background investigations include a polygraph examination. The components of a background investigation may also vary by agency. For example, the

investigative elements of a background investigation for a Top Secret level clearance with the Federal Bureau of Investigation may differ from the investigative elements of a background investigation for a Top Secret level clearance with the Department of Health and Human Services. Also see the section of this report titled "On Average, How Long Does it Take to Obtain a Security Clearance?"

[26] See U.S. General Accounting Office (now, the U.S. Government Accountability Office), *More Accurate Estimate of Overdue Security Clearance Reinvestigations is Needed*, GAO/T-NSIAD-00-246, September 20, 2000, p. 1, at http://gao.gov/assets/110/108657.pdf. Also see U.S. Government Accountability Office, *Personnel Security Clearances: Continuing Leadership and Attention Can Enhance Momentum Gained from Reform Effort*, GAO-12-815T, June 21, 2012, at http://gao.gov/assets/600/591784.pdf.

[27] Ibid. Also see DOD Defense Security Service publication "Industrial Personnel Security Clearance Process," at http://www.dss.mil/psmo-i/indus_psmo-i_process_applicant.html.

[28] Ibid. In some instances, if the individual is a former government employee or had previously performed work as a contractor for the government, he or she may already hold an active security clearance at the necessary level. In such cases, the agency may accept the individual's existing clearance, or the agency may request an additional background investigation. See the section of this report titled "May a Security Clearance Granted by One Agency Be Accepted by Other Agencies?"

[29] This includes background investigations conducted as part of the process for granting a security clearance and investigations conducted as part of a suitability determination. See http://www.opm.gov/investigations/background- investigations.

[30] See U.S. Senate Committee on Homeland Security and Governmental Affairs, Subcommittee on Efficiency and Effectiveness of Federal Programs and the Federal Workforce and Subcommittee on Financial and Contracting Oversight, *Safeguarding our Nation's Secrets: Examining the Security Clearance Process*, hearing, 113th Congress, 1st sess., June 20, 2013.

[31] Ibid. Information on USIS is available at http://www.usis.com/investigations.aspx. A price list for the investigative services that USIS offers through the General Services Administration's (GSA's) Federal Supply Schedule is available at https://www. gsaadvantage.gov/ref_text/GS22F9736H/0L6B9C.2JF5M9_GS-22F-9736H_USIS738X27. PDF .

[32] See Federal Procurement Data System, at https://www.fpds.gov/fpdsng_cms. Information on CACI, OMNI, and Keypoint are available at http://www.caci.com/fcc/ILS, http://omniplex.com/investigative.cfm, and http://www.keypoint.us.com/Solutions/ Investigative, respectively. GSA Schedule price lists for CACI, OMNI, and Keypoint are available at https://www.gsaadvantage.gov /ref_text/GS02F0179N/0GN3TD.20SEF2_GS-02F- 0179N_0179NSUPP6BA20090625. PDF, https://www.gsaadvantage.gov/ref_text/ GS15 F0051L/ 0KBU9A.2F3S1B_GS15 F0051L_GS-15F-0051L-3-6-2012-693979.PDF, and https://www.gsaadvantage.gov /ref_text/ GS02F0054S/0LM2RS.2M4L2C_ GS02F0054S_GS-02F-0054S-4-16-2013-884762.PDF, respectively.

[33] U.S. Department of Justice, Office of the Inspector General, Evaluation and Inspections Division, *Review of the Department's Contractor Personnel Security Process*, March 2013, p. 4, at http://www.justice.gov/oig/reports/2013/ e1303.pdf.

[34] Office of the Director of National Intelligence, *2012 Report on Security Clearance Determinations*, p. 5.

[35] Ibid.

[36] According to the testimony of Stephen Lewis, Deputy Director, Security Directorate, Office of the Under Secretary of Defense (Intelligence), the costs for background investigations of individuals employed by companies who contract with DOD are paid for by the department and not the contractor because "analysis shows that if we were to allow the contractors to build [the cost of those clearances] into the contract ... then they would add overhead on the management of that, so the most cost-effective way was to manage it from the department. We pay those costs, because we pay it either way." U.S. Senate Committee on Homeland

Security and Governmental Affairs, Subcommittee on Efficiency and Effectiveness of Federal Programs and the Federal Workforce and Subcommittee on Financial and Contracting Oversight, *Safeguarding our Nation's Secrets: Examining the Security Clearance Process*.

[37] A summary of the investigative products offered by OPM-FIS is available at http://www.opm.gov/investigations/ background-investigations/reference/annual-report-for-fiscal-year-2012.pdf.

[38] For example, the cost of an initial background investigation for certain "moderate risk" positions that require a Confidential or Secret level clearance may range from $752 to $809, while the cost of an initial background investigation for positions that require a Top Secret level clearance range from $4,005 to $4,399. Additional "à la carte" services, such as Bar Association license checks, are also offered by OPM-FIS at little or no additional cost. OPM's Investigations Reimbursable Billing Rates for FY2013 are available at http://www.opm.gov/investigations/ background-investigations/federal-investigations-notices/2012/fin12-07.pdf. OPM's "Position Designation Tool," which provides agencies with guidelines for determining the type of investigation required for certain government and contractor positions, is available at http://archive.opm.gov/investigate/resources/ position/ Position%20Designation%20System%20October%202010.pdf.

[39] Possible options for appealing the outcome of a security clearance investigation and adjudication are discussed in more detail below. See the section of this report titled "Can the Outcome of a Security Clearance Determination Be Appealed?"

[40] Office of the Director of National Intelligence, *2012 Report on Security Clearance Determinations*, April 12, 2013, p. 6, at http://www.dni.gov/files/documents/ 2012%20Report%20on%20Security%20Clearance%20Determinations%20Final.pdf.

[41] Office of Director of National Intelligence, *IRTPA Title III Annual Report for 2010*, February 15, 2011, p. 2, at http://www.dni.gov/files/documents/Newsroom/Reports%20and%20Pubs/ Security%20Clearance%20Determination_Report.pdf. Title III of the Intelligence Reform and Terrorism Prevention Act (IRTPA) of 2004 required the ODNI to report annually on the processing times for security clearances through February 2011. For this reason, the *Annual Report for 2010* is the final (and the most recent) IRTPA report published.

[42] These guidelines apply to "all United States Government civilian and military personnel, consultants, contractors, employees of contractors, licensees, certificate holders or grantees and their employees and other individuals who require access to classified information." 32 C.F.R. § 147.1.

[43] 32 C.F.R. §§ 147.3-147.15.

[44] 32 C.F.R. § 147.2(d).

[45] Ibid.

[46] For example, having associates who are connected with a foreign government is a condition that may cause a security concern under "foreign influence." The security concern may be mitigated, however, if those contacts were the result of official U.S. government business. 32 C.F.R. § 147.4.

[47] For example, Intelligence Community Policy Guidance Number 704.3, which applies to agencies within the Intelligence Community (as defined in the National Security Act of 1947), establishes policies and procedures for appealing a denial or revocation of access to SCI. Office of the Director of National Intelligence, *Denial or Revocation of Access to Sensitive Compartmented Information, Other Controlled Access Program Information, and Appeals Processes*, October 2, 2008, at http://www.dni.gov/files/documents/ICPG/ icpg_704_3.pdf.

[48] For example, FBI policy allows an applicant to appeal the results of certain pre-employment and personnel security polygraph examinations. U.S. Department of Justice, Office of the Inspector General, Evaluations and Inspections Division, *Use of Polygraph Examinations in the Department of Justice*, I-2006-008, September 2006, pp. 44-50, at http://www.justice. gov/oig/reports/plus/e0608/final.pdf.

[49] For example, see Office of the Inspector General of the Department of Defense, Deputy Inspector General for Intelligence, *DoD Security Clearance Adjudication and Appeal Process*, December 12, 2003, pp. 7-12, at http://www.dodig.mil/Ir/reports/fy04/04-INTEL-02.pdf.

[50] Elizabeth L. Newman, *Security Clearance Law and Procedure*, 2nd ed. (Arlington, VA: Dewey Publications, 2008), p. 13.

[51] P.L. 108-458.

[52] See, for example, *Security Clearance Reform—Upgrading the Gateway to the National Security Community*, House Permanent Select Committee on Intelligence, H.Rept. 110-916, November 20, 2008; Charles B. Sowell, Deputy Assistant Director for Special Security, Office of the Director of National Intelligence, for Senate Homeland Security and Government Affairs Committee hearing on Security Clearance Changes, June 21, 2012; and *Personnel Security Clearance, Progress Has Been Made to Improve Timeliness but Continued Oversight Is Needed to Sustain Momentum*, The Government Accountability Office, November 2010. GAO-11-65, p. 27, at http://www.gao.gov/products/GAO-11- 65.

In: NSA Intelligence Collection, Leaks … ISBN: 978-1-62948-937-7
Editor: Simon Cepeda

Chapter 3

CRIMINAL PROHIBITIONS ON THE PUBLICATION OF CLASSIFIED DEFENSE INFORMATION*

Jennifer K. Elsea

SUMMARY

The publication of classified information related to National Security Agency (NSA) surveillance activity is the latest in a series of leaks to the press that has riveted Congress's attention. Press reports describing classified U.S. operations abroad have led to calls from Congress for an investigation into the source of the leaks, and Attorney General Holder appointed two special prosecutors to look into the matter. The online publication of classified defense documents and diplomatic cables by the organization WikiLeaks and subsequent reporting by the *New York Times* and other news media had already focused attention on whether such publication violates U.S. criminal law. The source of the WikiLeaks material, Army Private Bradley Manning, has been sentenced to 35 years' imprisonment for a number of offenses under the Uniform Code of Military Justice (UCMJ), but was not convicted of aiding the enemy. A grand jury in Virginia is deciding whether to indict any civilians in connection with the disclosure. A number of other cases involving

* This is an edited, reformatted and augmented version of a Congressional Research Service publication, CRS Report for Congress R41404, prepared for Members and Committees of Congress, from www.crs.gov, dated September 9, 2013.

charges under the Espionage Act, including efforts to extradite Edward Snowden in connection with the leak of NSA documents pertaining to certain surveillance programs, demonstrate the Obama Administration's relatively hardline policy with respect to the prosecution of persons suspected of leaking classified information to the media.

This report identifies some criminal statutes that may apply to the publication of classified defense information, noting that these have been used almost exclusively to prosecute individuals with access to classified information (and a corresponding obligation to protect it) who make it available to foreign agents, or to foreign agents who obtain classified information unlawfully while present in the United States. While prosecutions appear to be on the rise, leaks of classified information to the press have relatively infrequently been punished as crimes, and we are aware of no case in which a publisher of information obtained through unauthorized disclosure by a government employee has been prosecuted for publishing it. There may be First Amendment implications that would make such a prosecution difficult, not to mention political ramifications based on concerns about government censorship. To the extent that the investigation implicates any foreign nationals whose conduct occurred entirely overseas, any resulting prosecution may carry foreign policy implications related to the exercise of extraterritorial jurisdiction and whether suspected persons may be extradited to the United States under applicable treaty provisions.

This report discusses the statutory prohibitions that may be implicated, including the Espionage Act; the extraterritorial application of such statutes; and the First Amendment implications related to such prosecutions against domestic or foreign media organizations and associated individuals. The report provides a summary of previous legislative efforts to criminalize the unauthorized disclosure of classified information.

INTRODUCTION

The online publication of classified defense documents and diplomatic cables by the organization WikiLeaks and subsequent reporting by the *New York Times*, *The Guardian* (UK), and *Der Spiegel* (Germany), among others, focused attention on whether such publication violates U.S. criminal law. The source of the material, Army Private Bradley Manning, has been sentenced to 35 years' imprisonment for a number of offenses under the Uniform Code of Military Justice (UCMJ). A grand jury has been empanelled in Alexandria, VA, to investigate civilian involvement in the matter,[1] but information regarding the targets of the investigation and the prosecution's theory of the case remains under seal.[2]

Another set of newspaper stories reporting on U.S. covert or clandestine operations overseas led to calls for the appointment of a special prosecutor to investigate executive branch leaks.[3] In June 2012, Attorney General Eric Holder appointed two U.S. Attorneys to lead FBI investigations into certain possible unauthorized disclosures, but did not reveal which news stories were thought to have reported leaked material.[4] The Federal Bureau of Investigation (FBI) had reportedly opened investigations into the disclosure of information leading to a news story about the United States' alleged involvement in deploying a computer virus to damage uranium enrichment facilities in Iran[5] and another to look into a report about a foiled terrorist plot.[6] Other news accounts regarding, for example, the use of unmanned aerial vehicles (also known as drones) for targeted killings abroad[7] have likewise given rise to questions about whether White House officials discuss classified information with journalists, but the scope of the investigations remains unclear.

The publication of classified information related to National Security Agency (NSA) surveillance activity is the latest in a series of leaks to the press that has riveted Congress's attention.

At this stage in these investigations, there is little public information available. Accordingly, the following discussion provides a general overview of the relevant law as it may apply to pertinent allegations reported in the media, assuming them to be true. The discussion should not be interpreted to confirm the truth of any allegations or establish that a particular statute has been violated.

BACKGROUND

The WikiLeaks Releases

WikiLeaks.org has described itself as a "public service designed to protect whistle-blowers, journalists and activists who have sensitive materials to communicate to the public."[8] Arguing that "[p]rincipled leaking has changed the course of history for the better," it stated that its purpose is to promote transparency in government and fight corporate fraud by publishing information governments or corporations would prefer to keep secret, obtained from sources in person, by means of postal drops, and by using "cutting-edge cryptographic technologies" to receive material electronically.[9] The organization has promised contributors that their anonymity will be protected.

According to press reports, WikiLeaks obtained more than 91,000 secret U.S. military reports related to the war in Afghanistan and posted the majority of them, unredacted, on its website in late July 2010, after first alerting the *New York Times* and two foreign newspapers, the *Guardian* (London) and *Der Spiegel* (Germany), about the pending disclosure.[10] Military officials charged an Army private, Bradley Manning, for offenses related to the provision of documents to WikiLeaks.[11] Private Manning, a dual U.S.-British citizen, was already in military custody under suspicion of having provided WikiLeaks with video footage of an airstrike that resulted in the deaths of civilians.[12] He was convicted by court-martial and sentenced to 35 years' imprisonment, reduction in rank, forfeiture of pay, and a dishonorable discharge.[13]

Private Manning was acquitted of the most serious charge he faced, aiding the enemy in violation of UCMJ Article 104.[14] The violation is a capital offense, but prosecutors did not seek the death penalty.[15] Aiding the enemy is also one of two offenses under the UCMJ that apply to "any person," rather than "any person subject to [chapter 47 of Title 10, *U.S. Code*]" as defined in UCMJ Article 2,[16] which might have raised the possibility that civilians who are not connected with the military could be similarly charged. There has been no suggestion that court-martial of any civilians has been considered in connection with the disclosure, and such a prosecution would likely be subject to constitutional challenge. Private Manning had pleaded guilty to some lesser offenses without the benefit of a plea agreement with prosecutors,[17] and defended his actions as motivated by a desire to enlighten the public.[18]

U.S. officials condemned the leaks, predicting that the information disclosed could lead to the loss of lives of U.S. soldiers in Afghanistan and Afghan citizens who have provided them assistance.[19] Defense Secretary Robert M. Gates informed members of Congress that a preliminary review of the disclosed information by the Defense Department found that no sensitive information related to intelligence sources or methods was made public, but reiterated that the release of Afghan informants' names could have "potentially dramatic and grievously harmful consequences."[20] WikiLeaks subsequently released some 400,000 documents related to the war in Iraq,[21] this time with names of informants apparently redacted.[22]

In late November 2010, WikiLeaks began publishing what the *New York Times* calls a "mammoth cache of a quarter-million confidential American diplomatic cables," dated for the most part from 2008-2010.[23] WikiLeaks.org posted 220 cables on November 28, 2010, as a first installment, some of which were redacted to protect diplomatic sources. The most recent documents in the collection are reportedly dated February 2010,[24] but some of them apparently go back several decades.[25]

The United States government was aware of the impending disclosure, although not apparently directly informed by the web-based anti-secrecy organization (or given access to the documents to be released). WikiLeaks Editor in Chief Julian Assange, in a letter sent to the U.S. Ambassador to the UK, Louis Susman, offered to consider any U.S. requests to protect specific information that the government believes could, if published, put any individuals at significant risk of harm.[26] The State Department Legal Adviser responded in a letter to Mr. Assange's attorney that the publication of classified materials violates U.S. law, that the United States will not negotiate with WikiLeaks with respect to the publication of illegally obtained classified documents, and that WikiLeaks should cease these activities and return all documents, as well as delete any classified U.S. government material in its possession from its databases.[27] Mr. Assange responded by accusing the United States of adopting a confrontational stance and indicating an intent to continue publishing the materials, subject to the checks WikiLeaks and its media partners planned to implement to reduce any risk to individuals.[28]

After learning the classified cables were to be published, the Defense Department notified the U.S. Senate and House Armed Services Committees in general terms about what to expect.[29] DOD Assistant Secretary for Legislative Affairs Elizabeth King explained that "State Department cables by their nature contain everyday analysis and candid assessments that any government engages in as part of effective foreign relations," and predicted that the publication of the classified cables, which she described as intended to "wreak havoc and destabilize global security," could potentially jeopardize lives.[30] State Department spokesman Philip J. Crowley told *Bloomberg* that the State Department was "assessing the possible impact on our on-going diplomatic activity and notifying both Congress and other governments what may occur."[31] The White House issued a statement condemning the activities of WikiLeaks[32] and ordered all agencies to conduct reviews of their information security policies and programs.[33]

As of early January 2011, about 1% of the cables had been published, with WikiLeaks.org posting only those cables that had already been released by the newspapers, as redacted by the newspapers.[34] The State Department warned human rights activists, foreign government officials, and businesspeople who are identified in the diplomatic cables that they may be at risk, although their names had not been published thus far, and relocated a few of them for their safety.[35] The cables continued to be released at an apparently steady rate,[36] until it was discovered in late August 2011, that the entire unredacted file had been published on the web along with the password needed to access the data.[37] WikiLeaks then began publishing the remaining documents at a much faster pace, so that all of the more than 250,000 diplomatic cables are accessible without redactions on the Internet.[38]

Other Leaks Prosecutions

The Obama Administration is taking a relatively hardline stance with respect to those suspected of leaking classified information to the press, with seven prosecutions currently under way or completed (including Bradley Manning).[39] A former National Security Agency (NSA) official, Thomas A. Drake, recently agreed to plead guilty to exceeding authorized use of a government computer in violation of 18 U.S.C. Section 1030(a)(2)(B) (a misdemeanor), after the government dropped more serious charges under the Espionage Act, among other offenses.[40] Mr. Drake was initially investigated beginning in 2007 in connection with the *New York Times*' revelations regarding the Bush Administration's warrantless surveillance program, but was eventually charged in connection with providing classified information that revealed alleged NSA mismanagement to the *Baltimore Sun*.[41] The prosecution eventually dropped these charges after the judge ruled that the government's proposed substitutions for documentary evidence it sought to introduce would not provide an adequate opportunity for the defendant to present his case.[42] After calling the government's treatment of the defendant in the case "unconscionable" and declining to impose a fine, the court sentenced Mr. Drake to one year probation and 240 hours of community service.[43]

A guilty plea was also secured in a case against an FBI contract linguist accused of providing secret documents to a blogger.[44] The defendant, Shamai Kedem Leibowitz, was sentenced to 20 months in prison for violation of 18 U.S.C. Section 798 by passing five documents classified at the "secret" level in relation to communications intelligence.[45]

The Obama Administration is seeking to compel *New York Times* reporter James Risen to testify at the trial of former CIA officer Jeffrey Sterling, who is accused of providing classified information to Mr. Risen that formed the basis of part of a book.[46] The judge ruled, however, that Mr. Risen need only testify about certain non-privileged information and need not identify the source of the material in question.[47] The government asked the court to reconsider the ruling, arguing that the reporter's testimony is "qualitatively different" from the circumstantial evidence the judge thought would suffice to establish the same facts,[48] but the court declined to reconsider.

The Court of Appeals for the Fourth Circuit reversed the ruling on appeal,[49] holding there is neither a First Amendment privilege nor a federal common-law privilege protecting journalists from being compelled to testify.[50] The government also prevailed in its appeal of an order striking two of its primary witnesses for failure to produce information about them to the defense in a timely manner.[51]

Another ongoing prosecution involved a former State Department contractor who was indicted in 2010 for disclosing national defense information to Fox News reporter James Rosen, related to intelligence regarding North Korea's nuclear weapons program.[52] Mr. Rosen was apparently also investigated and named as a co-conspirator in the indictment, but was not himself indicted for his role.[53] The contractor, Stephen Kim, was at the time of the disclosure a senior adviser for intelligence detailed to the State Department's arms control compliance bureau.[54] The court denied the defendant's motions to dismiss the espionage charges based on the Constitution's Treason Clause as well as the First and Fifth Amendments.[55]

A former CIA officer, John Kiriakou, was charged for the unauthorized disclosure of classified information to a journalist. Because the disclosures were alleged to have included the identities of covert CIA employees, he was also charged under the rarely used Intelligence Identities Protection Act.[56] After the judge rejected his Espionage Act defense based on the lack of intent to harm the United States or give advantage to a foreign nation,[57] Mr. Kiriakou pleaded guilty to violating the Intelligence Identities Protection Act.[58]

Most recently, Edward Snowden, a former contractor employee working as a computer system administrator at an NSA facility in Hawaii, was charged in connection with leaking top secret documents related to certain NSA programs to the *Guardian* (UK) and the *Washington Post*.[59] He permitted the newspapers to publish his name, but fled to Hong Kong before he could be taken into custody. He is reportedly seeking asylum in Ecuador.[60] The criminal complaint against him charges two violations of the Espionage Act and theft of government property.[61]

The publication of the leaked documents by WikiLeaks and the subsequent reporting of information contained therein, as well as other publications of "leaked" classified information, raise questions with respect to the possibility of bringing criminal charges for the dissemination of materials by media organizations following an unauthorized disclosure, in particular when done by non-U.S. nationals overseas. This report discusses the statutory prohibitions that may be implicated; the extraterritorial application of such statutes; and the First Amendment implications related to such prosecutions against domestic or foreign media organizations and associated individuals.

Statutory Protection of Classified Information

While there is no one statute that criminalizes the unauthorized disclosure of any classified information, a patchwork of statutes exists to protect information depending upon its nature, the identity of the discloser and of those to whom it was disclosed, and the means by which it was obtained. It seems likely that most of the information disclosed by WikiLeaks that was obtained from Department of Defense databases falls under the general rubric of information related to the national defense. The diplomatic cables obtained from State Department channels may also contain information relating to the national defense and thus be covered under the Espionage Act, but otherwise their disclosure by persons who are not government employees does not appear to be directly proscribed.[62] It is possible that some of the government information disclosed in any of the releases does not fall under the express protection of any statute, despite its classified status.

The Espionage Act

National defense information in general is protected by the Espionage Act,[63] 18 U.S.C. Sections 793–798, while other types of relevant information are covered elsewhere. Some provisions apply only to government employees or others who have authorized access to sensitive government information,[64] but many apply to all persons. 18 U.S.C. Section 793 prohibits the gathering, transmitting, or receipt of defense information with the intent or reason to believe the information will be used against the United States or to the benefit of a foreign nation. Violators are subject to a fine or up to 10 years' imprisonment, or both,[65] as are those who conspire to violate the statute.[66]

Persons who possess defense information that they have reason to know could be used to harm the national security, whether the access is authorized or unauthorized, and who disclose that information to any person not entitled to receive it, or who fail to surrender the information to an officer of the United States, are subject to the same penalty.[67] Although it is not necessary that the information be classified by a government agency, the courts seem to give deference to the executive determination of what constitutes "defense information."[68] Information that is made available by the government to the public is not covered under the prohibition, however, because public availability of such information negates the bad-faith intent requirement.[69] On the other hand, classified documents remain within the ambit of the statute even if information contained therein is made public by an unauthorized leak.[70]

18 U.S.C. Section 794 (aiding foreign governments or communicating information to an enemy in time of war) covers "classic spying" cases,[71] providing for imprisonment for any term of years or life, or under certain circumstances, the death penalty.[72] The provision penalizes anyone who transmits defense information to a foreign government (or foreign political or military party) with the intent or reason to believe it will be used against the United States. It also prohibits attempts to elicit information related to the public defense "which might be useful to the enemy."[73] The death penalty is available only upon a finding that the offense resulted in the death of a covert agent or directly concerns nuclear weapons or other particularly sensitive types of information. The death penalty is also available under Section 794 for violators who gather, transmit or publish information related to military plans or operations and the like during time of war, with the intent that the information reach the enemy.[74] These penalties are available to punish any person who participates in a conspiracy to violate the statute. Offenders are also subject to forfeiture of any ill-gotten gains and property used to facilitate the offense.[75]

The unauthorized creation, publication, sale or transfer of photographs or sketches of vital defense installations or equipment as designated by the President is prohibited by 18 U.S.C. Sections 795 and 797.[76] Violators are subject to fine or imprisonment for not more than one year, or both.

The knowing and willful disclosure of certain classified information is punishable under 18 U.S.C. Section 798 by fine and/or imprisonment for not more than 10 years.[77] To incur a penalty, the disclosure must be prejudicial to the safety or interests of the United States or work to the benefit of any foreign government and to the detriment of the United States. The provision applies only to information related to cryptographic systems or communications intelligence that is specially designated by a U.S. government agency for "limited or restricted dissemination or distribution."[78]

Members of the military[79] who commit espionage, defined similarly to the conduct prohibited in 18 U.S.C. Section 794, may be tried by court-martial for violating Article 106a of the Uniform Code of Military Justice (UCMJ),[80] and sentenced to death if certain aggravating factors are found by unanimous determination of the panel.[81] Unlike offenses under Section 794, Article 106a offenses need not have resulted in the death of a covert agent or involve military operations during war to incur the death penalty. One of the aggravating factors enabling the imposition of the death penalty under Article 106a is that "[t]he accused has been convicted of another offense involving espionage or treason for which either a sentence of death or imprisonment for life was authorized by statute."

However, the government is not limited to charging the offense of espionage under Article 106a, discussed above. Members could also be tried by court-martial for violations of Article 92, failure to obey order or regulation,[82] Article 104, aiding the enemy,[83] or under the general article, Article 134.[84] Article 134 offenses include "all disorders and neglects to the prejudice of good order and discipline in the armed forces, all conduct of a nature to bring discredit upon the armed forces, and crimes and offenses not capital"[85] that are not enumerated elsewhere in the UCMJ. Specifically, clause 3 of Article 134 (crimes and offenses not capital) may be utilized to try a member of the military for a violation of applicable federal law, such as 18 U.S.C. Section 1030(a) discussed below, not addressed by the UCMJ.

Other Statutes

18 U.S.C. Section 1030(a)(1) punishes the willful retention, communication, or transmission, etc., of classified information retrieved by means of knowingly accessing a computer without (or in excess of) authorization, with reason to believe that such information "could be used to the injury of the United States, or to the advantage of any foreign nation." Receipt of information procured in violation of the statute is not addressed, but depending on the specific facts surrounding the unauthorized access, criminal culpability might be asserted against persons who did not themselves access a government computer as conspirators, aiders and abettors, or accessories after the fact.[86] The provision imposes a fine or imprisonment for not more than 10 years, or both, in the case of a first offense or attempted violation. Repeat offenses or attempts can incur a prison sentence of up to 20 years.

18 U.S.C. Section 641 punishes the theft or conversion of government property or records for one's own use or the use of another. While this section does not explicitly prohibit disclosure of classified information, it has been used to prosecute "leakers."[87] Violators may be fined, imprisoned for not more than 10 years, or both, unless the value of the property does not exceed the sum of $100, in which case the maximum prison term is one year. The statute also covers knowing receipt or retention of stolen or converted property with the intent to convert it to the recipient's own use. It does not appear to have been used to prosecute any recipients of classified information even where the original discloser was charged under the statute.

50 U.S.C. Section 3121 provides for the protection of information concerning the identity of covert intelligence agents.[88] It generally covers persons authorized to know the identity of such agents or who learn the identify of covert agents as a result of their general access to classified information,[89] but can also apply to a person who learns of the identity of a covert agent through a "pattern of activities intended to identify and expose covert agents" and discloses the identity to any individual not authorized access to classified information, with reason to believe that such activities would impair U.S. foreign intelligence efforts. For those without authorized access, the crime is subject to a fine or imprisonment for a term of not more than three years. To be convicted, a violator must have knowledge that the information identifies a covert agent whose identity the United States is taking affirmative measures to conceal. To date, there have been no reported cases interpreting the statute, but it did result in two convictions pursuant to guilty pleas.[90]

18 U.S.C. Section 1924 prohibits the unauthorized removal of classified material by government employees, contractors, and consultants who come into possession of the material by virtue of their employment by the government.[91] The provision imposes a fine of up to $1,000 and a prison term up to one year for offenders who knowingly remove material classified pursuant to government regulations concerning the national defense or foreign relations of the United States, with the intent of retaining the materials at an unauthorized location.[92]

There appears to be no statute that generally proscribes the acquisition or publication of diplomatic cables, although government employees who disclose such information without proper authority may be subject to prosecution. 18 U.S.C. Section 952 punishes employees of the United States who, without authorization, willfully publish or furnish to another any official diplomatic code or material prepared in such a code, by imposing a fine, a prison sentence (up to 10 years), or both. The same punishment applies for materials "obtained while in the process of transmission between any foreign government and its diplomatic mission in the United States,"[93] but not, apparently, materials obtained during transmission from U.S. diplomatic missions abroad to the State Department or vice versa (unless the material was or purports to have been prepared using an official diplomatic code—it is unclear whether messages that are encrypted for transmission are covered). The removal of classified material concerning foreign relations with the intent to store them at an unauthorized location is a misdemeanor under 18 U.S.C. Section 1924, which also applies only to U.S. government employees.

50 U.S.C. Section 783 penalizes government officers or employees who, without proper authority, communicate classified information to a person whom the employee has reason to suspect is an agent or representative of a foreign government.[94] It is also unlawful for the representative or agent of the foreign government to receive classified information.[95] Violation of either of these provisions is punishable by a fine of up to $10,000 or imprisonment for not more than 10 years.[96] Violators are thereafter prohibited from holding federal public office.[97] Violators must forfeit all property derived directly or indirectly from the offense and any property that was used or intended to be used to facilitate the violation.[98]

Analysis

In light of the foregoing, it seems that there is ample statutory authority for prosecuting individuals who elicit or disseminate many of the documents at issue, as long as the intent element can be satisfied and potential damage to national security can be demonstrated.[99] There is some authority, however, for interpreting 18 U.S.C. Section 793, which prohibits the communication, transmission, or delivery of protected information to anyone not entitled to possess it, to exclude the "publication" of material by the media.[100] Publication is not expressly proscribed in 18 U.S.C. Section 794(a), either, although it is possible that publishing covered information in the media could be construed as an "indirect" transmission of such information to a foreign party, as long as the intent that the information reach said party can be demonstrated.[101] The death penalty is available under that subsection if the offense results in the identification and subsequent death of "an individual acting as an agent of the United States,"[102] or the disclosure of information relating to certain other broadly defined defense matters. The word "publishes" does appear in 18

U.S.C. Section 794(b), which applies to wartime disclosures of information related to the "public defense" that "might be useful to the enemy" and is in fact intended to be communicated to the enemy. The types of information covered seem to be limited to military plans and information about fortifications and the like, which may exclude data related to purely historical matters.

Moreover, the statutes described in the previous section have been used almost exclusively to prosecute individuals with access to classified information (and a corresponding obligation to protect it) who make it available to foreign agents, or to foreign agents who obtain classified information unlawfully while present in the United States. While prosecutions appear to be on the rise, leaks of classified information to the press have not often been punished as crimes. CRS is aware of no case in which a publisher of information obtained through unauthorized disclosure by a government employee has been prosecuted for publishing it. There may be First Amendment implications that would make such a prosecution difficult, not to mention political ramifications based on concerns about government censorship. To the extent that the investigation implicates any foreign nationals whose conduct occurred entirely overseas, any resulting prosecution may carry foreign policy implications related to the exercise of extraterritorial jurisdiction and whether suspected persons may be extradited to the United States under applicable treaty provisions.

JURISDICTIONAL REACH OF RELEVANT STATUTES

The Espionage Act gives no express indication that it is intended to apply extraterritorially, but courts have not been reluctant to apply it to overseas conduct of Americans, in particular because Congress in 1961 eliminated a provision restricting the act to apply only "within the admiralty and maritime jurisdiction of the United States and on the high seas, as well as within the United States."[103] This does not answer the question whether the act is intended to apply to foreigners outside the United States. Because espionage is recognized as a form of treason,[104] which generally applies only to persons who owe allegiance to the United States, it might be supposed that Congress did not regard it as a crime that could be committed by aliens with no connection to the United States. However, the only court that appears to have addressed the question concluded otherwise.[105] A district court judge held in 1985 that a citizen of East Germany could be prosecuted under Sections

793(b), 794(a) and 794(c) for having (1) unlawfully sought and obtained information regarding the U.S. national defense, (2) delivered that information to his own government, and (3) conspired to do so with the intent that the information be used to the injury of the United States or to the advantage of the German Democratic Republic, all of which offenses were committed within East Germany or in Mexico. The court rejected the defendant's contention that construing the act to cover him would permit the prosecution of noncitizens "who might merely have reviewed defense documents supplied to them by their respective governments."[106] The court considered the scenario unlikely, stating, "Under the statutorily defined crimes of espionage in §§793 and 794, noncitizens would be subject to prosecution only if they actively sought out and obtained or delivered defense information to a foreign government or conspired to do so."[107]

Under this construction, it is possible that noncitizens involved in publishing materials disclosed to them by another would be subject to prosecution only if it can be demonstrated that they took an active role in obtaining the information. The case was not appealed. The defendant, Dr. Alfred Zehe, pleaded guilty in February, 1985 and was sentenced to eight years in prison, but was traded as part of a "spy swap" with East Germany in June of that year.[108]

Application of the Espionage Act to persons who do not hold a position of trust with the government, outside of the classic espionage scenario (in which an agent of a foreign government delivers damaging information to such hostile government), has been controversial. The only known case of that type involved two pro-Israel lobbyists in Washington, Steven J. Rosen and Keith Weissman, associated with the American Israel Public Affairs Committee (AIPAC), who were indicted in 2005 for conspiracy to disclose national security secrets to unauthorized individuals, including Israeli officials, other AIPAC personnel, and a reporter for the *Washington Post.*[109] Their part in the conspiracy amounted to receiving information from government employees with knowledge that the employees were not authorized to disclose it.[110] The prosecution was criticized for effectively "criminalizing the exchange of information,"[111] based in part on the government's theory that the defendants were guilty of solicitation of classified information because they inquired into matters they knew their government informant was not permitted to discuss, something that many journalists consider to be an ordinary part of their job.[112] Charges were eventually dropped, reportedly due to a judge's ruling regarding the government's burden of proving the requisite intent and concerns that classified information would have to be disclosed at trial.[113] With respect to the intent requirement, the judge interpreted the term "willfully" in connection with the phrase "reason to believe could be used to the injury of the United States" to require that the prosecution must prove that the defendant disclosed the information "with a bad faith purpose to either harm the United States or to aid a foreign government."[114] Later courts confronting the intent issue have differentiated this case to conclude that the "reason to believe" standard does not require an intent to do harm.[115]

EXTRADITION ISSUES[116]

There may be several legal obstacles to the extradition of such a suspect to the United States to face charges under the Espionage Act,[117] including the possibility that the crime constitutes a political offense for which extradition is unavailable. Extradition to or from the United States is almost exclusively a creature of treaty. The United States has extradition treaties with more than 100 countries, although there are many countries with which it does not.[118] In addition to providing an explicit list of crimes for which extradition may be granted, most modern extradition treaties also identify various classes of offenses and situations for which extradition may or must be denied.

The "political offense" exception has been a common feature of extradition treaties for almost a century and a half, and the exception appears to be contained in every modern U.S. extradition treaty.[119] A political offense may be characterized as a *pure political offense*, or one that is directed singularly at a sovereign entity and does not have the features an ordinary crime (e.g., there is no violation of the private rights of individuals),[120] or as a *relative political offense*, meaning an "otherwise common crime[] committed in connection with a political act ... or common crimes ... committed for political motives or in a political context."[121]

The political offense exception may pose a significant obstacle to the extradition of a person to the United States to face charges under the Espionage Act. Espionage, along with treason and sedition, has been recognized as a quintessential example of a purely political offense,[122] although this recognition may arguably apply only to the "classic case" of espionage on behalf of a foreign government by one who owes allegiance to the aggrieved government.[123] Even if the political offense exception applies to the unauthorized disclosure of national defense information, however, the United States could still seek the extradition of a suspect to face other criminal charges (though it would likely be unable to try the fugitive for an offense other than the one for which he was extradited),[124] although extradition might be refused if the charged conduct is deemed to have been committed in furtherance of an act of espionage (or other political offense).[125]

Extradition is also generally limited to crimes identified in the relevant treaty. Early extradition treaties concluded by the United States typically listed specific crimes constituting extraditable offenses.[126] Due in part to their vintage, these agreements did not address criminal offenses related to the dissemination or misuse of defense information. More recent agreements often adopt a dual criminality approach, in which extradition is available when each party recognizes a particular form of misconduct as a punishable offense (subject to other limitations found elsewhere in the applicable extradition treaty).[127] No U.S. extradition treaty currently in force lists espionage as an extraditable offense.[128] Assuming for the sake of argument that certain offenses under the Espionage Act are not *per se* political offenses for which extradition may not be granted, it would appear that the United States could only seek the extradition of a person for an espionage offense if the applicable treaty authorized extradition in cases of dual criminality, and the requested state recognized espionage (or perhaps unauthorized receipt or disclosure of protected government information) as a criminal offense under its domestic laws.

Whether extradition is available for an offense occurring outside the United States may depend in part upon whether the applicable treaty covers extraterritorial offenses. As a general rule, crimes are defined by the laws of the place where they are committed.[129] Nations have always been understood to have authority to outlaw and punish conduct occurring outside the confines of their own territory under some circumstances, but the United States now claims more sweeping extraterritorial application for some of its criminal laws than is recognized either in its more historic treaties or by many of today's governments.[130] This may complicate any extradition efforts because many U.S. extradition treaties apply only to crimes "committed within the [territorial] jurisdiction" of the country seeking extradition.[131] Some contemporary treaties call for extradition regardless of where the offense was committed, while perhaps an equal number permit or require denial of an extradition request that falls within an area where the countries hold conflicting views on extraterritorial jurisdiction.[132]

The extradition of a foreign national to the United States to face criminal charges may be impeded by nationality provisions contained in extradition treaties with many countries, which recognize the right of a requested party to refuse to extradite its own nationals. U.S. extradition agreements generally are either silent with respect to nationality, in which case all persons are subject to extradition without regard to their nationality, or they contain a nationality clause that specifies that parties are not bound to deliver up their own nationals, in some cases leaving room for executive discretion.[133] Some newer treaties declare that "extradition shall not be refused based on the nationality of the person sought," while others limit the nationality exemption to nonviolent crimes or bar nationality from serving as the basis to deny extradition when the fugitive is sought in connection with a listed offense. In some instances, an extradition treaty does expressly allow a country to refuse to extradite its nationals, but subsequent changes to a party's domestic laws have barred it from honoring requests for the extradition of its subjects.

The ability of the United States to obtain the extradition of a fugitive for a criminal offense may also be impacted by the existence of competing extradition requests made by other states. The criteria used by a requested state to determine the precedence given to competing extradition requests may be established either by its domestic laws or via its extradition treaties with the requesting countries.[134] If the requested state opts to give priority to the extradition request of another country, it might still be possible for the United States to obtain the extradition of the fugitive at a later date. Whether a fugitive extradited to one state can thereafter be extradited to a third country may depend upon the applicable treaties between the relevant states. Some extradition agreements authorize the requesting state to re-extradite a person to a third country in certain circumstances. Generally, re-extradition is only permitted when the state from whom extradition was initially obtained consents to the re-extradition of the fugitive, or the fugitive voluntarily remains in the state where he was initially extradited for a specified period after having been released from custody.[135]

CONSTITUTIONAL ISSUES

The publication of information pertaining to the national defense or foreign policy may serve the public interest by providing citizens with information necessary to shed light on the workings of government, but it seems widely accepted that the public release of at least some of such information poses a significant enough threat to the security of the nation that the public interest is better served by keeping it secret. The Constitution protects the public right to access government information and to express opinions regarding the functioning of the government, among other things, but it also charges the government with "providing for the common defense." Policymakers are faced with the task of balancing these interests.

The First Amendment to the U.S. Constitution provides: "Congress shall make no law ... abridging the freedom of speech, or of the press...."[136] Despite this absolute language, the Supreme Court has held that "[t]he Government may ... regulate the content of constitutionally protected speech in order to promote a compelling interest if it chooses the least restrictive means to further the articulated interest."[137]

Where speech is restricted based on its content, the Supreme Court generally applies "strict scrutiny," which means that it will uphold a content-based restriction only if it is necessary "to promote a compelling interest," and is "the least restrictive means to further the articulated interest."[138] Protection of the national security from external threat is without doubt a compelling government interest.[139] It has long been accepted that the government has a compelling need to suppress certain types of speech, particularly during time of war or heightened risk of hostilities.[140] Speech likely to incite immediate violence, for example, may be suppressed.[141] Speech that would give military advantage to a foreign enemy is also susceptible to government regulation.[142]

Where First Amendment rights are implicated, it is the government's burden to show that its interest is sufficiently compelling to justify enforcement. Whether the government has a compelling need to punish disclosures of classified information turns on whether the disclosure has the potential of causing damage to the national defense or foreign relations of the United States.[143] Actual damage need not be proved, but potential damage must be more than merely speculative and incidental.[144] On the other hand, the Court has stated that "state action to punish the publication of truthful information seldom can satisfy constitutional standards."[145] And it has described the constitutional purpose behind the guarantee of press freedom as the protection of "the free discussion of governmental affairs."[146]

Although information properly classified in accordance with statute or executive order carries by definition, if disclosed to a person not authorized to receive it, the potential of causing at least identifiable harm to the national security of the United States,[147] it does not necessarily follow that government classification by itself will be dispositive of the issue in the context of a criminal trial. However, courts have adopted as an element of the espionage statutes a requirement that the information at issue must be "closely held."[148] Government classification will likely serve as strong evidence to support that contention, even if the information seems relatively innocuous or does not contain much that is not already publicly known.[149] Typically, courts have been unwilling to review decisions of the executive related to national security, or have made a strong presumption that the material at issue is potentially damaging.[150] Still, judges have recognized that the government must make *some* showing that the release of specific national defense information has the potential of harming U.S. interests, lest the Espionage Act become a means to punish whistle-blowers who reveal information that poses more of a danger of embarrassing public officials than of endangering national security.[151]

The Supreme Court seems satisfied that national security is a vital interest sufficient to justify some intrusion into activities that would otherwise be protected by the First Amendment—at least with respect to federal employees. Although the Court has not held that government classification of material is sufficient to show that its release is damaging to the national security,[152] it has seemed to accept without much discussion the government's assertion that the material in question is damaging. It is unlikely that a defendant's bare assertion that information poses no danger to U.S. national security will be persuasive without some convincing evidence to that effect, or proof that the information is not closely guarded by the government.[153]

A challenge to the Espionage Act has reached the Supreme Court for decision in only one instance. In *Gorin v. United States*,[154] the Court upheld portions of the act now codified as 18 U.S.C. Sections 793 and 794 against assertions of vagueness, but only because jury instructions properly established the elements of the crimes, including the scienter requirement (proof of "guilty knowledge") and a definition of "national defense" that includes potential damage in case of unauthorized release of protected information and materials. *Gorin* was a "classic case" of espionage, and did not involve a challenge based on the First Amendment right to free speech. The Court agreed with the government that the term "national defense" was not vague; it was satisfied that the term describes "a generic concept of broad connotations, referring to the military and naval establishments and the related activities of national preparedness."[155] Whether information was "related to the national defense" was a question for the jury to decide,[156] based on its determination that the information "may relate or pertain to the usefulness, efficiency or availability of any of the above places, instrumentalities or things for the defense of the United States of America. The connection must not be a strained one nor an arbitrary one. The relationship must be reasonable and direct."[157] As long as the jury was properly instructed that only information likely to cause damage meets the definition of information "related to the national defense" for the purpose of the statute, the term was not unconstitutionally vague.

United States v. Morison[158] is significant in that it represents the first case in which a person was convicted for selling classified documents to the media.[159] Samuel Loring Morison, charged with providing classified satellite photographs to the British defense periodical *Jane's Defence Weekly*, argued that the espionage statutes did not apply to his conduct because he could not have had the requisite intent to commit espionage. The U.S. Court of Appeals for the Fourth Circuit rejected his appeal, finding the intent to sell photographs that he clearly knew to be classified sufficient to satisfy the scienter requirement under 18 U.S.C. Section 793(d) (disclosure by lawful possessor of defense information to one not entitled to receive it). The definition of "relating to the national defense" was held not to be overbroad because the jury had been instructed that the government had the burden of showing that the information was so related.[160] His assertedly laudable motive in permitting publication of the photographs was not found to negate the element of intent.[161]

The fact that the Morison prosecution involved a leak to the media with no obvious intent to transmit sensitive information to hostile intelligence services did not persuade the jury or the judges involved that he lacked culpability. The Justice Department did, however, come under some criticism on the basis that such prosecutions are so rare as to amount to a selective prosecution in his case, and that it raised concerns about the chilling effect such prosecutions could have on would-be whistle-blowers who could provide information embarrassing to the government but vital to public discourse.[162] On leaving office, President Clinton pardoned Morison.[163]

As far as the possible prosecution of the publisher of information leaked by a government employee is concerned, the most relevant case is likely to be the *Pentagon Papers* case.[164] To be sure, the case involved an injunction against publication rather than a prosecution for having published information, but the rationale for protecting such disclosure may nevertheless inform any decision involving a conviction. In a *per curiam* opinion accompanied by nine concurring or dissenting opinions, the U.S. Supreme Court refused to grant the government's request for an injunction to prevent the *New York Times* and the *Washington Post* from printing a classified study of the U.S. involvement in Vietnam. The Court explained:

> prior restraints are the most serious and least tolerable infringement on First Amendment rights.... A prior restraint, ... by definition, has an

> immediate and irreversible sanction. If it can be said that a threat of criminal or civil sanctions after publication "chills" speech, prior restraint "freezes" it at least for the time. The damage can be particularly great when the prior restraint falls upon the communication of news and commentary on current events.[165]

A majority of the Justices suggested in separate *dicta* that the newspapers—along with the former government employee who leaked the documents to the press—could be prosecuted under the Espionage Act.[166] Still, in later cases the Court stressed that any prosecution of a publisher for what has already been printed would have to overcome only slightly less insurmountable hurdles.[167] Moreover, if national security interests were not sufficient to outweigh the First Amendment principles implicated in the prior restraint of pure speech related to the public interest, as in the *Pentagon Papers* case,[168] it is difficult to discern an obvious rationale for finding that punishing that same speech after it has already been disseminated nevertheless tilts the balance in favor of the government's interest in protecting sensitive information.

The publication of truthful information that is lawfully acquired enjoys considerable First Amendment protection.[169] The Court has not resolved the question "whether, in cases where information has been acquired *unlawfully* by a newspaper or by a source, government may ever punish not only the unlawful acquisition, but the ensuing publication as well."[170] (The *Pentagon Papers* Court did not consider whether the newspapers' receipt of the classified document was in itself unlawful, although it appeared to accept that the documents had been unlawfully taken from the government by their source.)

The Court has established that "routine newsgathering" is presumptively lawful acquisition, the fruits of which may be published without fear of government retribution.[171] However, what constitutes "routine newsgathering" has not been further elucidated. In the 2001 case *Bartnicki v. Vopper*, the Court cited the *Pentagon Papers* case to hold that media organizations cannot be punished (albeit in the context of civil damages) for divulging information on the basis that it had been obtained unlawfully by a third party.[172] The holding suggests that recipients of unlawfully disclosed information cannot be considered to have obtained such material unlawfully based solely on their knowledge (or "reason to know") that the discloser acted unlawfully. Under such circumstances, disclosure of the information by the innocent recipient would be covered by the First Amendment, although a wrongful disclosure by a person in violation of an obligation of trust would receive no First

Amendment protection, regardless of whether the information was obtained lawfully.[173] *Bartnicki* had to do with the disclosure of illegally intercepted communications in violation of federal and state wiretap laws, which prohibited disclosure of such information by anyone who knew or had reason to know that it was the product of an unlawful interception, but did not prohibit the *receipt* of such information. The Espionage Act, by contrast, does expressly prohibit the receipt of certain national defense material with knowledge or reason to believe that it "has been or will be obtained, taken, made, or disposed of" contrary to the provisions of the act.[174] This distinction could possibly affect whether a court would view the information as having been lawfully acquired; although the *Bartnicki* opinion seems to establish that knowledge that the information was unlawfully disclosed by the initial leaker cannot by itself make receipt or subsequent publication unlawful, it does not directly address whether knowledge of the nature of the information received would bring about a different result.

Prior Legislative Efforts

The current laws protecting classified information have been criticized as a patchwork of mostly outdated provisions that are vague and inconsistent, or that they may not cover all the information the government legitimately needs to protect.[175] Conversely, others argue that they fail to take due consideration of the value of releasing to the public information that the government would prefer to keep out of view.[176]

The Classified Information Protection Act of 2001

In 2000, and again in 2001-2002, Congress sought to create 18 U.S.C. Section 798A, subsection (a) of which would have read:

> Whoever, being an officer or employee of the United States, a former or retired officer or employee of the United States, any other person with authorized access to classified information, or any other person formerly with authorized access to classified information, knowingly and willfully discloses, or attempts to disclose, any classified information acquired as a result of such person's authorized access to classified information to a person (other than an officer or employee of the United States) who is not authorized access to such classified information, knowing that the person

> is not authorized access to such classified information, shall be fined under this title, imprisoned not more than 3 years, or both.[177]

The proposed provision would have penalized the disclosure of any material designated as classified for any reason related to national security, regardless of whether the violator intended that the information be delivered to and used by foreign agents (in contrast to 50 U.S.C. Section 783). It would have been the first law to penalize disclosure of information to entities other than foreign governments or their equivalent solely because it is classified, without a more specific definition of the type of information covered.[178] In short, the provision would have made it a crime to disclose or attempt to disclose classified information[179] to any person who does not have authorized access to such information, with exceptions covering disclosures to Article III courts, or to the Senate or House committees or Members, and for authorized disclosures to persons acting on behalf of a foreign power (including an international organization). The provision would have amended the espionage laws in Title 18 by expanding the scope of information they cover. The proposed language was intended to make it easier for the government to prosecute unauthorized disclosures of classified information, or "leaks" of information that might not amount to a violation of current statutes. The language was intended to ease the government's burden of proof in such cases by eliminating the need "to prove that damage to the national security has or will result from the unauthorized disclosure,"[180] substituting a requirement to show that the unauthorized disclosure was of information that "is or has been properly classified" under a statute or executive order.

The 106th Congress passed the measure as part of the Intelligence Authorization Act for Fiscal Year 2001,[181] but President Clinton vetoed it, calling it "well-intentioned" as an effort to deal with legitimate concerns about the damage caused by unauthorized disclosures, but "badly flawed" in that it was "overbroad" and posed a risk of "unnecessarily chill[ing] legitimate activities that are at the heart of a democracy."[182] President Clinton explained his view that

> [a] desire to avoid the risk that their good faith choice of words—their exercise of judgment—could become the subject of a criminal referral for prosecution might discourage Government officials from engaging even in appropriate public discussion, press briefings, or other legitimate official activities. Similarly, the legislation may unduly restrain the ability of former Government officials to teach, write, or engage in any activity aimed at building public understanding of complex issues.

> Incurring such risks is unnecessary and inappropriate in a society built on freedom of expression and the consent of the governed and is particularly inadvisable in a context in which the range of classified materials is so extensive. In such circumstances, this criminal provision would, in my view, create an undue chilling effect.[183]

The 107th Congress considered passing an identical provision,[184] but instead directed the Attorney General and heads of other departments to undertake a review of the current protections against the unauthorized disclosure of classified information, and to issue a report recommending legislative or administrative actions.[185] An identical measure was introduced late in the 109th Congress, but was not reported out of committee.[186]

The Attorney General, in his report to the 108th Congress, concluded that

> [a]lthough there is no single statute that provides criminal penalties for all types of unauthorized disclosures of classified information, unauthorized disclosures of classified information fall within the scope of various current statutory criminal prohibitions. It must be acknowledged that there is no comprehensive statute that provides criminal penalties for the unauthorized disclosure of classified information irrespective of the type of information or recipient involved. Given the nature of unauthorized disclosures of classified information that have occurred, however, I conclude that current statutes provide a legal basis to prosecute those who engage in unauthorized disclosures, if they can be identified. It may be that carefully drafted legislation specifically tailored to unauthorized disclosures of classified information generally, rather than to espionage, could enhance our investigative efforts. The extent to which such a provision would yield any practical additional benefits to the government in terms of improving our ability to identify those who engage in unauthorized disclosures of classified information or deterring such activity is unclear, however.[187]

Recent Legislative Activity

The House of Representatives included a provision in the National Defense Authorization Act for FY2013 (H.R. 4310), passed by the House on May 18, 2012, to require the Attorney General to initiate an investigation into possible violations of federal law regarding the disclosure of "sensitive information involving the military, intelligence, and operational capabilities of the United States and Israel," and to report on the status of the investigation no later than 60 days after enactment, Section 1099C. However, the measure was replaced in conference with a sense of the Congress expressing concern about damage to the national security that may be caused by unauthorized disclosures, suggesting that federal agencies should take steps to address the problem if they have not already done so, and recommending that the Justice Department investigate leaks and prosecute those responsible, Section 1080.

Several other bills were introduced during the 112th Congress to address the protection of classified information. The Securing Human Intelligence and Enforcing Lawful Dissemination Act ("SHIELD Act"), S. 315,[188] and a companion bill in the House, H.R. 703,[189] would have amended 18 U.S.C. Section 798 to add coverage for disclosures of classified information related to human intelligence activities (the statute currently covers only certain information related to communications intelligence). The bills would also have added "transnational threat" to the entities whose benefit from unlawful disclosures would make such disclosures illegal.

The Espionage Statutes Modernization Act of 2010, S. 355,[190] would have broadened the Espionage Act provisions by extending their coverage to all classified information related to the national security (rather than merely national defense information), and would incorporate non-state threats into the prohibition by substituting "foreign power" (as defined under the Foreign Intelligence Surveillance Act, at 50 U.S.C. Section 1801) for "foreign government" or "foreign nation." The bill also included a new provision to prohibit the intentional unauthorized disclosure of properly classified information by government employees, contractors, or consultants in violation of the terms of a nondisclosure agreement. H.R. 1823, the Criminal Code Modernization and Simplification Act of 2011, would have overhauled the Espionage Act along with the rest of Title 18, *U.S. Code*. Chapter 15, subchapter E of the proposed criminal code would have replaced the Espionage Act with three sections, one applicable to the gathering of defense information or its transmission to any person not entitled to receive it, if done with the intent or reason to believe it "will be used to the injury of the United States, or to the advantage of any foreign power." Another section would have applied only to those having lawful possession or control of defense information who recklessly permit it to be lost, stolen, or destroyed, or fail to report such an eventuality to an appropriate superior officer. The final section would have prohibited the knowing disclosure of classified or similarly protected information to a person not entitled to receive it, or the use of such information to the injury of the United States or the advantage of a foreign power. The substitution of "foreign power" (as defined in the Foreign

Intelligence Surveillance Act) for "foreign government" is perhaps the most noteworthy change from the Espionage Act as currently in force.

CONCLUSION

The Espionage Act on its face applies to the receipt and unauthorized dissemination of national defense information, which has been interpreted broadly to cover closely held government materials related to U.S. military operations, facilities, and personnel. It has been interpreted to cover the activities of foreign nationals overseas, at least when they take an active part in seeking out information. Although cases involving disclosures of classified information to the press have been rare, it seems clear that courts have regarded such disclosures by government employees to be conduct that enjoys no First Amendment protection, regardless of the motives of the divulger or the value the release of such information might impart to public discourse.[191] The Supreme Court has stated, however, that the question remains open whether the publication of unlawfully obtained information by the media can be punished consistent with the First Amendment. Thus, although unlawful acquisition of information might be subject to criminal prosecution with few First Amendment implications, the publication of that information remains protected. Whether the publication of national security information can be punished likely turns on the value of the information to the public weighed against the likelihood of identifiable harm to the national security, arguably a more difficult case for prosecutors to make.

End Notes

[1] Scott Shane, Supporter of Leak Suspect Is Called Before Grand Jury, NY TIMES, June 16, 2011, at 22. After the Attorney General indicated in December 2010 that he had authorized investigators to take "significant" steps with respect to the WikiLeaks case (but declined to elaborate), an attorney for Julian Assange told news reporters that he had learned from Swedish authorities that a grand jury had been empanelled in Alexandria, VA, to investigate the matter. See Charlie Savage, Building Case For Conspiracy By WikiLeaks, NY TIMES, December 16, 2010, at 1. The attorney reportedly told Al-Jazeera in an interview that Julian Assange is at least one target of the investigation. See Assange attorney: Secret grand jury meeting in Virginia on WikiLeaks, CNN.COM, December 13, 2010, http://articles.cnn.com/2010-12-13/justice/wikileaks.investigation_1_julian-assange-wikileaks-case-grand-jury?_s=PM:CRIME. However, another of Assange's attorneys refuted the claim, stating Assange's legal team has no concrete evidence that a grand jury is considering charges

against Assange. Justin Elliot, Assange grand jury report "purely speculation", WAR ROOM (December 14, 2010), http://www.salon.com/news/politics/war_room/2010/12/14/ assange_grand_jury_rumors/ index.html. Separate from the grand jury investigation, the U.S. Attorney for the Eastern District of Virginia reportedly subpoenaed records of several persons from the social media network Twitter. See Scott Shane and John F. Burns, Twitter Records in Wikileaks Case are Subpoenaed, NY TIMES, January 9, 2011, at 1.

[2] Based on a letter accompanying a grand jury subpoena, there is some speculation that federal prosecutors are pursuing a conspiracy theory under the Espionage Act of 1917 as well as laws prohibiting misuse of government computers and misappropriation of government property. See Ellen Nakashima and Jerry Markon, Documents Offer Hints of U.S. Legal Strategy in WikiLeaks Investigation, WASH. POST, April 29, 2011, at A3. It is believed that a conspiracy theory will permit prosecutors to pursue charges on the basis of activities not subject to First Amendment protection. See Shane, supra footnote 1 (quoting attorney Abbe D. Lowell).

The subpoena has been posted at http://www.salon.com/news/opinion/glenn_greenwald/ 2011/06/09/wikileaks/ subpoena.pdf. The letter accompanying the subpoena can be viewed at http://www.salon.com/news/opinion/ glenn_greenwald/2011/06/09 /wikileaks/ Ltr.House.pdf. It appears to be a form letter that advises recipients that the grand jury is investigating "possible violations of federal criminal law, but not necessarily limited to conspiracy to" commit violations of 18 U.S.C. §793(g) (espionage), 18 U.S.C. §371 (general conspiracy statute; fraud against the government), 18 U.S.C. §1030 (computer fraud), and 18 U.S.C. §641 (conversion of public property).

[3] See Evan Perez, Holder Puts Top Prosecutors on Leak Probe, WALL ST. J., June 9, 2012, at A6 (reporting some accusations that the Obama Administration has itself permitted selective leaks of classified information in order to enhance the President's reelection prospects).

[4] See Press Release, U.S. Department of Justice Office of Public Affairs, Assignment of U.S. Attorneys to Lead Investigations of Possible Unauthorized Disclosures of Classified Information (June 8, 2012), available at http://www.justice.gov/opa/pr/2012/June/12-ag-736.html.

[5] See David E. Sanger, Obama Order Sped Up Wave of Cyberattacks Against Iran, NY Times, June 1, 2012, at A1, available at http://www.nytimes.com/2012/06/01/world/middleeast/ obama-ordered-wave-of-cyber attacks-againstiran.html?pagewanted=1&_r=1&hp. The reporting was based, according to the author, "on interviews over the past 18 months with current and former American, European and Israeli officials involved in the program" and other experts, none of whom were willing to allow names to be printed because of the classified nature of the program.

[6] See Scott Shane and Eric Schmitt, Qaeda Foiled in Plot to Plant Redesigned Bomb on Plane, U.S. Officials Say, NY Times, May 8, 2012, at A12.

[7] See, e.g., Jo Becker and Scott Shane, Secret 'Kill List' Proves a Test Of Obama's Principles and Will, NY TIMES, May 29, 2012, at A1.

[8] http://www.wikileaks.org/wiki/WikiLeaks:About.

[9] Id.

[10] The New York Times published a series of articles under the headline "The War Logs," which is available online at http://www.nytimes.com/interactive/world/war-logs.html. The Times describes the leaked material as an archive covering six years of incident reports and intelligence documents—"usually spare summaries but sometimes detailed narratives"—that "illustrate[s] in mosaic detail why" the military effort in Afghanistan has not weakened the Taliban. C. J. Chivers et al., The Afghan Struggle: A Secret Archive, N.Y. TIMES, July

26, 2010, at 1. The German periodical Der Spiegel published a series of articles under the topic "Afghanistan Protocol," which is available (in English) online at http://www.spiegel.de/international/world/0,1518,708314,00.html. The Guardian (UK) published a series entitled "Afghanistan: The War Logs," which is available online at http://www.guardian.co.uk/world/the-war-logs.

[11] See Ed Pilkington, Bradley Manning May Face Death Penalty, GUARDIAN (UK), March 3, 2011, available at http://www.guardian.co.uk/world/2011/mar/03/bradley-manning-may-face-death-penalty (reporting that 22 new charges, including aiding the enemy, were added to the original twelve specifications).

[12] Military airstrike video leak suspect in solitary confinement, CNN.com, August 1, 2010, available at http://www.cnn.com/2010/POLITICS/07/31/wikileaks.manning/index.html.

[13] Charlie Savage and Emmarie Huetteman, Manning Sentenced to 35 Years for a Pivotal Leak of U.S. Files, NY TIMES, August 21, 2013, at A1.

[14] 10 U.S.C. §904.

[15] See Jim Miklaszewski and Courtney Kube, Manning faces new charges, possible death penalty, MSNBC.com, May 3, 2011, available at http://www.msnbc.msn.com/id/41876046/ns/us_news-security/.

[16] 10 U.S.C. §802. The only UCMJ offense that applies more broadly than to persons subject to UCMJ jurisdiction under Article 2 is spying, Article 106 (10 U.S.C. §106), which applies to "any person ... in time of war."

[17] Charlie Savage, Private Accused of Leaks Offers Partial Guilty Plea, NY TIMES, November 8, 2012.

[18] Charlie Savage, Soldier Admits Providing Files to Wikileaks, NY TIMES, February 28, 2013.

[19] Admiral Michael Mullen, Chairman of the Joint Chiefs of Staff, on Meet the Press, August 1, 2010, transcript available at http://www.msnbc.msn.com/id/38487969/ns/meet_the_press-transcripts/.

[20] See Elisabeth Bumiller, Gates Found Cost of Leaks Was Limited, NY TIMES, October 17, 2010 (quoting letter to Senator Levin from Secretary Gates).

[21] See The Iraq Archive: The Strands of a War, NY TIMES, at http://www.nytimes.com/2010/10/23/world/middleeast/ 23intro.html?_r=1.

[22] See Anna Mulrine, Wikileaks Iraq Documents not as Damaging as Pentagon Feared—Yet, CHRISTIAN SCIENCE MONITOR, October 25, 2010. The New York Times has stated it redacted names prior to publishing the leaked materials. See The Iraq Archive, supra footnote 21.

[23] State's Secrets, NY TIMES (online edition), November 29, 2010, http://www.nytimes.com/interactive/world/ statessecrets.html. According to the Guardian, the fact that most of the cables are dated from 2008 to 2009 is explained by the increase in the number of U.S. embassies linked to the military's secure computer network, SIPRNet, over the past decade. See The US embassy cables, GUARDIAN (UK), http://www.guardian.co.uk/news/datablog/2010/nov/29/ wikileaks-cables-data.

[24] Scott Shane and Andrew W. Lehren, Cables Obtained by WikiLeaks Shine Light Into Secret Diplomatic Channels, NY TIMES.

[25] The Guardian states that the earliest of the cables is from 1966. See The US embassy cables, supra footnote 23.

[26] Letter to Ambassador Susman, November 26, 2010, available at http://documents.nytimes.com/letters-betweenwikileaks-and-gov.

[27] Letter from State Department Legal Adviser Harold Hongju Koh to Jennifer Robinson, November 27, 2010, available at http://documents.nytimes.com/letters-between-wikileaks-and-gov.

[28] Letter to Ambassador Susman, November 28, 2010, available at http://documents.nytimes.com/letters-betweenwikileaks-and-gov.

[29] Tony Capaccio, Pentagon Alerts House, Senate Panels to New Classified WikiLeaks Release, BLOOMBERG, November 24, 2010, http://www.bloomberg.com/news/2010-11-24/pentagon-warns-house-senate-defense-panels-ofmore-wikileaks-documents.html.

[30] Id.

[31] Id.

[32] White House, Statement of the Press Secretary, November 28, 2010, at http://www.whitehouse.gov/the-press-office/ 2010/11/28/statement-press-secretary. The statement reads in full:

We anticipate the release of what are claimed to be several hundred thousand classified State department cables on Sunday night that detail private diplomatic discussions with foreign governments. By its very nature, field reporting to Washington is candid and often incomplete information. It is not an expression of policy, nor does it always shape final policy decisions. Nevertheless, these cables could compromise private discussions with foreign governments and opposition leaders, and when the substance of private conversations is printed on the front pages of newspapers across the world, it can deeply impact not only US foreign policy interests, but those of our allies and friends around the world. To be clear—such disclosures put at risk our diplomats, intelligence professionals, and people around the world who come to the United States for assistance in promoting democracy and open government. These documents also may include named individuals who in many cases live and work under oppressive regimes and who are trying to create more open and free societies. President Obama supports responsible, accountable, and open government at home and around the world, but this reckless and dangerous action runs counter to that goal. By releasing stolen and classified documents, Wikileaks has put at risk not only the cause of human rights but also the lives and work of these individuals. We condemn in the strongest terms the unauthorized disclosure of classified documents and sensitive national security information.

[33] Memorandum from Jacob J. Lew, Director, Office of Management and Budget to Heads of Executive Departments and Agencies (November 28, 2010), at http://www.whitehouse.gov/sites/default/files/omb/memoranda/2011/m11- 06.pdf. For other White House responses to the WikiLeaks disclosures, see FACT SHEET: U.S. Government Mitigation Efforts in Light of the Recent Unlawful Disclosure of Classified Information (December 1, 2010), at http://www.whitehouse.gov/search/site/classified%20information.

[34] See Mark Landler and Scott Shane, U.S. Sends Warning to People Named in Cable Leaks, N.Y. TIMES, January6, 2011.

[35] Id.

[36] For information related to the content of the cables, see Wikileaked: Inside the State Department's Secret Cables, FOREIGN POL'Y, http://wikileaks.foreignpolicy.com/; The US embassy cables, supra footnote 23.

[37] See Kim Zetter, U.S. Sources Exposed as Unredacted State Department Cables Are Unleashed Online, THREAT LEVEL (September 1, 2011, 3:22 PM), http://www.wired.com/threatlevel/2011/09/wikileaks-unredacted-cables/.

[38] See Scott Shane, Spread of Leaked Cables on Web Prompts Dispute, NY Times, September 1, 2011, available at http://www.nytimes.com/2011/09/02/us/02wikileaks.html?_r=1.

[39] See Scott Shane, Ex-N.S.A. Official Takes Plea Deal, NY TIMES, June 10, 2011, at A1, available at http://www.nytimes.com/2011/06/10/us/10leak.html?_r=1.

[40] See Ellen Nakashima, Ex-NSA official Thomas Drake to plead guilty to misdemeanor, WASH. POST, June 9, 2011, at http://www.washingtonpost.com/national/national-security/ex-nsa-manager-has-reportedly-twice-rejected-pleabargains-in-espionage-act-case/2011/06/09/AG89ZHNH_story.html.

[41] See Jane Mayer, The Secret Sharer, New Yorker, May 23, 2011, http://www. newyorker. com/reporting/2011/05/23/ 110523fa_fact_mayer.

[42] United States v. Drake, Crim. No. 10 CR 00181 RDB (N.D. Md.) (Government Motion to Dismiss the Indictment at the Time of Sentencing) (filed June 10, 2011), available at http://www.fas.org/sgp/jud/drake/061011-dismiss.pdf.

[43] See Steven Aftergood, Handling of Drake Leak Case was "Unconscionable," Court Said, SECRECY NEWS (July 29, 2011), http://www.fas.org/blog/secrecy/2011/07/ drake_ transcript.html.

[44] See Press Release, Department of Justice, Former FBI Contract Linguist Pleads Guilty to Leaking Classified Information to Blogger (December 17, 2009), available at http://www.justice.gov/opa/pr/2009/December/09-nsd1361.html.

[45] Id.

[46] Jeffrey Sterling was indicted for several counts of violating the Espionage Act (disclosure and retention of national defense information) as well as mail fraud, conversion of government property, and obstruction of justice. The indictment is available at http://www.fas.org/sgp/ jud/sterling/indict.pdf.

[47] Steven Aftergood, Reporter Risen Will Not Have to Identify Source in Leak Trial, SECRECY NEWS (August 1, 2011), http://www.fas.org/blog/secrecy/2011/08/risen_off_hook.html. For an overview of the law regarding the reporter's privilege, see CRS Report RL34193, Journalists' Privilege: Overview of the Law and Legislation in the 113th Congress, by Kathleen Ann Ruane.

[48] See Government's Motion for Clarification and Reconsideration, United States v. Sterling, No. 1:10cr485 (E.D. Va. August 24, 2011), available at http://www.fas.org/sgp/jud/sterling/ 082411-recon.pdf.

[49] United States v. Sterling, __ F.3d __, 2013 WL 3770692 (4th Cir. July 19, 2013).

[50] See CRS Report WSLG630, Confusing Branzburg: Is There a Journalists' Privilege Under the First Amendment?, by Kathleen Ann Ruane.

[51] Sterling at *22-*25.

[52] See Spencer S. Hsu, State Dept. contractor charged in leak to news organization, WASH. POST, August 28, 2010.

[53] Ann E. Marimow, A rare peek into a Justice Department leak probe, WASH. POST, May 19. 2013.

[54] See Hsu, supra, footnote 52.

[55] United States v. Kim, 808 F. Supp. 2d 44 (D.D.C. 2011).

[56] 50 U.S.C. §§421-426. For more information about this statute, see CRS Report RS21636, Intelligence Identities Protection Act, by Jennifer K. Elsea.

[57] United States v. Kiriakou, 2012 WL 4903319 (E.D. Va. October 16, 2012) (holding that the scienter requirement for violating the Espionage Act by disclosing intangible information requires the government to establish only that the possessor of the information had reason to believe that the information could be used to the injury of the United States or the advantage of any foreign nation).

[58] Press Release, U.S. Attorney for the Eastern District of Virginia, "Former CIA Officer John Kirakou Pleads Guilty to Disclosing Classified Information About CIA Officer," October 23, 2012, available at http://www.fbi.gov/ washingtondc/press-releases/2012/former-cia-officer-john-kirakou-pleads-guilty-to-disclosing-classified-informationabout-cia-officer.

[59] Mark Mazzetti and Michael S. Schmidt, Ex-Worker at C.I.A. Says He disclosed U.S. Surveillance, NY TIMES, June 10, 2013, at A1.

[60] Ellen Barry and Peter Baker, Snowden, in Russia, Seeks Asylum in Ecuador, NY TIMES, June 23, 2013, at A1.

[61] Peter Finn and Sari Horwitz, U.S. files charges against Snowden, WASH. POST, June 22, 2013, at A1 (reporting that DOJ officials have filed a criminal complaint).

[62] See 18 U.S.C. §952 (prohibiting the disclosure or publication of certain diplomatic material obtained "by virtue of ... employment by the United States").

[63] Act of October 6, 1917, ch. 106, §10(i), 40 Stat. 422.

[64] E.g., 18 U.S.C. §§952 (prohibiting disclosure of diplomatic codes and correspondence), 1924 (unauthorized removal and retention of classified documents or material); 50 U.S.C. §783 (unauthorized disclosure of classified information to an agent of a foreign government, unauthorized receipt by foreign government official).

[65] 18 U.S.C. §793(a)-(c) provides:

(a) Whoever, for the purpose of obtaining information respecting the national defense with intent or reason to believe that the information is to be used to the injury of the United States, or to the advantage of any foreign nation, goes upon, enters, flies over, or otherwise obtains information concerning any vessel, aircraft, work of defense, [etc.], or any prohibited place so designated by the President by proclamation in time of war or in case of national emergency in which anything for the use of the Army, Navy, or Air Force is being prepared or constructed or stored, information as to which prohibited place the President has determined would be prejudicial to the national defense; or

(b) Whoever, for the purpose aforesaid, and with like intent or reason to believe, copies, takes, makes, or obtains, or attempts to copy, take, make, or obtain any sketch, photograph, photographic negative, blueprint, plan, map, model, instrument, appliance, document, writing, or note of anything connected with the national defense; or

(c) Whoever, for the purpose aforesaid, receives or obtains or agrees or attempts to receive or obtain from any person, or from any source whatever, any [protected thing] connected with the national defense, knowing or having reason to believe ... that it has been or will be obtained, taken, made, or disposed of by any person contrary to the provisions of this chapter [18 U.S.C. §§792 et seq.]....

[66] 18 U.S.C. §793(g) provides:

If two or more persons conspire to violate any of the foregoing provisions of this section, and one or more of such persons do any act to effect the object of the conspiracy, each of the parties to such conspiracy shall be subject to the punishment provided for the offense which is the object of such conspiracy.

[67] 18 U.S.C. §793(e) provides:

Whoever having unauthorized possession of, access to, or control over any document [or other protected thing related to the national defense], or information relating to the national defense which information the possessor has reason to believe could be used to the injury of the United States or to the advantage of any foreign nation, willfully communicates, delivers, transmits ... to any person not entitled to receive it, or willfully retains the same and fails to deliver it to the officer or employee of the United States entitled to receive it; ... Shall be fined under this title or imprisoned not more than ten years, or both.

Section 793(d) is identical to §794(e), except that it applies to persons with authorized access to the information at issue, in which case the failure to deliver offense applies to failure to turn the information over to a government official only if there was a demand for its return.

Section 793(f) likewise applies only to those with authorized access to the covered materials, punishing those who

1. through gross negligence permits the same to be removed from its proper place of custody or delivered to anyone in violation of his trust, or to be lost, stolen, abstracted, or destroyed, or
2. having knowledge that the same has been illegally removed from its proper place of custody or delivered to anyone in violation of its trust, or lost, or stolen, abstracted, or destroyed, and fails to make prompt report of such loss, theft, abstraction, or destruction to his superior officer.

[68] The government must demonstrate that disclosure of a document is at least "potentially damaging" to the United States or advantageous to a foreign government. See United States v. Morison, 844 F.2d 1057, 1072 (4th Cir.), cert. denied, 488 U.S. (1988)(upholding conviction under 18 U.S.C. §793 for delivery of classified photographs to publisher). Whether the information is "related to the national defense" under this meaning is a question of fact for the jury to decide. Id. at 1073.At least one judge has held that in the case of a disclosure of intangible information, the government needs to prove only that the defendant has reason to believe that such information is potentially damaging, which, in the case of a person with access to classified information, can largely be inferred from the fact that information is classified. See United States v. Kiriakou, 2012 WL 4903319 at *1 (E.D. Va. October 16, 2012) (scienter requirement heightened in the case of disclosure of intangible national defense information); id. at *3 (noting that defendant was a "government employee trained in the classification system who could appreciate the significance of the information he allegedly disclosed").

[69] See Gorin v. United States, 312, U.S. 9, 27-28 (1941) ("Where there is no occasion for secrecy, as with reports relating to national defense, published by authority of Congress or the military departments, there can, of course, in all likelihood be no reasonable intent to give an advantage to a foreign government."). While Gorin dealt with a violation that required reason to believe materials obtained or transmitted were to be used to harm the United States or benefit a foreign nation, it seems likely that the public nature of information would also negate a reason to believe that its disclosure could harm U.S. national security for the purposes of 18 U.S.C. §793(d-e).

[70] United States v. Squillacote, 221 F.3d 542, 578 (4th Cir. 2000).

[71] Morison, 844 F.2d at 1064-65 (explaining that critical element distinguishing §794 from §793 is the requirement that disclosure be made to an agent of a foreign government rather than anyone not entitled to receive it).

[72] §794. Gathering or delivering defense information to aid foreign government

(a) Whoever, with intent or reason to believe that it is to be used to the injury of the United States or to the advantage of a foreign nation, communicates, delivers, or transmits ... to any foreign government, or to any faction or party or military or naval force within a foreign country, whether recognized or unrecognized by the United States, or to any representative, officer, agent, employee, subject, or citizen thereof, either directly or indirectly, any document [or other protected thing], or information relating to the national defense, shall be punished by death or by imprisonment for any term of years or for life, except that the sentence of death shall not be imposed unless the jury or ... the court, further finds that the offense resulted in the identification by a foreign power (as defined in section 101(a) of the Foreign Intelligence Surveillance Act of 1978 [50 U.C.S. §1801(a)]) of an individual acting as an agent of the United States and consequently in the death of that individual, or directly concerned nuclear weaponry, military spacecraft or satellites, early warning systems, or other means of defense or retaliation against large-scale attack; war plans; communications intelligence or cryptographic information; or any other major weapons system or major element of defense strategy.

[73] Section 794(b) provides:

(b) Whoever, in time of war, with intent that the same shall be communicated to the enemy, collects, records, publishes, or communicates, or attempts to elicit any information with respect to the movement, numbers, description, condition, or disposition of any of the Armed Forces, ships, aircraft, or war materials of the United States, or with respect to the plans or conduct, or supposed plans or conduct of any naval or military operations, or with respect to any works or measures undertaken for or connected with, or intended for the fortification or defense of any place, or any other information relating to the public defense, which might be useful to the enemy, shall be punished by death or by imprisonment for any term of years or for life....

[74] During time of war, any individual who communicates intelligence or any other information to the enemy may be prosecuted by the military for aiding the enemy under Article 104 of the Uniform Code of Military Justice (UCMJ), and if convicted, punished by "death or such other punishment as a court-martial or military commission may direct." 10 U.S.C. §904.

[75] 18 U.S.C. §794(d). Proceeds go to the Crime Victims Fund.

[76] §795. Photographing and sketching defense installations

(a) Whenever, in the interests of national defense, the President defines certain vital military and naval installations or equipment as requiring protection against the general dissemination of information relative thereto, it shall be unlawful to make any photograph, sketch, picture, drawing, map, or graphical representation of such vital military and naval installations or equipment without first obtaining permission of the commanding officer of the military or naval post, camp, or station, or naval vessels, military and naval aircraft, and any separate military or naval command concerned, or higher authority, and promptly submitting the product obtained to such commanding officer or higher authority for censorship or such other action as he may deem necessary....

§797. Publication and sale of photographs of defense installations

On and after thirty days from the date upon which the President defines any vital military or naval installation or equipment as being within the category contemplated under section 795 of this title [18], whoever reproduces, publishes, sells, or gives away any photograph, sketch, picture, drawing, map, or graphical representation of the vital military or naval installations or equipment so defined, without first obtaining permission of the commanding officer ... or higher authority, unless such photograph, sketch, picture, drawing, map, or graphical representation has clearly indicated thereon that it has been censored by the proper military or naval authority, shall be fined under this title or imprisoned not more than one year, or both.

[77] §798. Disclosure of classified information

(a) Whoever knowingly and willfully communicates, furnishes, transmits, or otherwise makes available to an unauthorized person, or publishes, or uses in any manner prejudicial to the safety or interest of the United States or for the benefit of any foreign government to the detriment of the United States any classified information—

a) concerning the nature, preparation, or use of any code, cipher, or cryptographic system of the United States or any foreign government; or
b) concerning the design, construction, use, maintenance, or repair of any device, apparatus, or appliance used or prepared or planned for use by the United States or any foreign government for cryptographic or communication intelligence purposes; or
c) concerning the communication intelligence activities of the United States or any foreign government; or
d) obtained by the processes of communication intelligence from the communications of any foreign government, knowing the same to have been obtained by such processes—

Shall be fined ... or imprisoned not more than ten years, or both.

[78] 18 U.S.C. §798(b).

[79] Persons subject to the UCMJ include members of regular components of the Armed Forces, cadets and midshipmen, members of reserve components while on training, members of the National Guard when in federal service, members of certain organizations when assigned to and serving the Armed Forces, prisoners of war, persons accompanying the Armed Forces in the field in time of war or a "contingency operation," and certain others with military status. 10 U.S.C. §802.

[80] 10 U.S.C. §906a(a) provides: Art. 106a. Espionage

(a)(1) Any person subject to [the UCMJ, chapter 47 of title 10, U.S.C.] who, with intent or reason to believe that it is to be used to the injury of the United States or to the advantage of a foreign nation, communicates, delivers, or transmits, or attempts to communicate, deliver, or transmit, to any entity described in paragraph (2), either directly or indirectly, anything described in paragraph (3) shall be punished as a court-martial may direct, except that if the accused is found guilty of an offense that directly concerns (A) nuclear weaponry, military spacecraft or satellites, early warning systems, or other means of defense or retaliation against large scale attack, (B) war plans, (C) communications intelligence or cryptographic information, or (D) any other major weapons system or major element of defense strategy, the accused shall be punished by death or such other punishment as a court-martial may direct.

(2) An entity referred to in paragraph (1) is—

a) a foreign government;
b) a faction or party or military or naval force within a foreign country, whether recognized or unrecognized by the United States; or
c) a representative, officer, agent, employee, subject, or citizen of such a government, faction, party, or force.

(3) A thing referred to in paragraph (1) is a document, writing, code book, signal book, sketch, photograph, photographic negative, blueprint, plan, map, model, note, instrument, appliance, or information relating to the national defense.

[81] 10 U.S.C. §906a(b)-(c).

[82] 10 U.S.C. §892.

[83] 10 U.S.C. §904.

[84] 10 U.S.C. §934.

[85] Id.

[86] Charges of conspiracy or aiding and abetting may be available with respect to any of the statutes summarized here, even if the statutes themselves do not mention such charges under the general conspiracy statute, 18 U.S.C. §371, or for aiding and abetting and the like under 18 U.S.C. §§2-4, unless otherwise made inapplicable. Some of the provisions that apply only to government employees or persons with authorized access to classified information

may therefore be applied to a broader set of potential violators. For more information about conspiracy law, see CRS Report R41223, Federal Conspiracy Law: A Brief Overview, by Charles Doyle.

[87] See United States v. Morison, 844 F.2d 1057 (4th Cir. 1988)(photographs and reports were tangible property of the government); United States v. Fowler, 932 F.2d 306 (4th Cir. 1991)("information is a species of property and a thing of value" such that "conversion and conveyance of governmental information can violate §641," citing United States v. Jeter, 775 F.2d 670, 680-82 (6th Cir. 1985)); United States v. Girard, 601 F.2d 69, 70-71 (2d Cir. 1979). The statute was used to prosecute a DEA official for leaking unclassified but restricted documents pertinent to an agency investigation. See Dan Eggen, If the Secret's Spilled, Calling Leaker to Account Isn't Easy, WASH. POST, October 3, 2003, at A5 (reporting prosecution of Jonathan Randel under conversion statute for leaking government documents to journalist).

[88] The Intelligence Identities and Protection Act of 1982, codified at 50 U.S.C. §§3121-26. For more information, see CRS Report RS21636, Intelligence Identities Protection Act, by Jennifer K. Elsea. The term "covert agent" is defined to include a non-U.S. citizen "whose past or present intelligence relationship to the United States is classified information and who is a present or former agent of, or a present or former informant or source of operational assistance to, an intelligence agency." 50 U.S.C. §3126(4)(c). "Intelligence agency" is defined to include a "foreign intelligence component of the Department of Defense"; informant means "any individual who furnishes information to an intelligence agency in the course of a confidential relationship." 50 U.S.C. §3126(5-6). The definitions suggest that the act is intended to protect the identities of persons who provide intelligence information directly to a military counterintelligence unit, but perhaps they can be read to cover those who provide information to military personnel carrying out other functions who provide situation reports intended to reach an intelligence component. In any event, the extraterritorial application of the statute is limited to U.S. citizens and permanent resident aliens. 50 U.S.C. §3124.

[89] Persons with direct access to information regarding the identities are subject to a prison term of not more than 15 years, while those who learn the identities through general access to classified information are subject to a term not greater than 10 years. 50 U.S.C. §3121. Charges of conspiracy, aiding and abetting, or misprision of felony are not available in connection with the offense, except in the case of a person who engaged in a pattern of activities to disclose the identities of covert agents or persons with authorized access to classified information. 50 U.S.C. §3122(b).

[90] See Richard B. Schmitt, Rare Statute Figures in Rove Case, LA TIMES, July 15, 2005, at A15 (reporting 1985 conviction of Sharon Scranage, a clerk for the CIA in Ghana, for disclosing identities of covert agents); Charlie Savage, Former C.I.A. Operative Pleads Guilty in Leak of Colleague's Name, NY TIMES, October 23, 2012.

[91] 18 U.C.S. §1924 provides:

a) Whoever, being an officer, employee, contractor, or consultant of the United States, and, by virtue of his office, employment, position, or contract, becomes possessed of documents or materials containing classified information of the United States, knowingly removes such documents or materials without authority and with the intent to retain such documents or materials at an unauthorized location shall be fined not more than $ 1,000, or imprisoned for not more than one year, or both.

b) For purposes of this section, the provision of documents and materials to the Congress shall not constitute an offense under subsection (a).

c) In this section, the term "classified information of the United States" means information originated, owned, or possessed by the United States Government concerning the national defense or foreign relations of the United States that has been determined pursuant to law or Executive order to require protection against unauthorized disclosure in the interests of national security.

[92] Id.

[93] 18 U.S.C. §952.

[94] 50 U.S.C. §783(a) provides:

Communication of classified information by Government officer or employee. It shall be unlawful for any officer or employee of the United States or of any department or agency thereof, or of any corporation the stock of which is owned in whole or in major part by the United States or any department or agency thereof, to communicate in any manner or by any means, to any other person whom such officer or employee knows or has reason to believe to be an agent or representative of any foreign government , any information of a kind which shall have been classified by the President (or by the head of any such department, agency, or corporation with the approval of the President) as affecting the security of the United States, knowing or having reason to know that such information has been so classified, unless such officer or employee shall have been specifically authorized by the President, or by the head of the department, agency, or corporation by which this officer or employee is employed, to make such disclosure of such information.

[95] 50 U.S.C. 783(b) provides:

Receipt of, or attempt to receive, by foreign agent or member of Communist organization, classified information. It shall be unlawful for any agent or representative of any foreign government knowingly to obtain or receive, or attempt to obtain or receive, directly or indirectly, from any officer or employee of the United States or of any department or agency thereof or of any corporation the stock of which is owned in whole or in major part by the United States or any department or agency thereof, any information of a kind which shall have been classified by the President (or by the head of any such department, agency, or corporation with the approval of the President) as affecting the security of the United States, unless special authorization for such communication shall first have been obtained from the head of the department, agency, or corporation having custody of or control over such information.

[96] 50 U.S.C. §783(c).

[97] Id.

[98] 50 U.S.C. §783(e).

[99] It appears the intent element varies depending on the provision. In general, it is satisfied by proof that the material was obtained or disclosed willfully "with intent or reason to believe that the information is to be used [or could be used] to the injury of the United States, or to the advantage of any foreign nation." 18 U.S.C. §§793 and 794. This has been interpreted to require the prosecution to demonstrate a "bad purpose." See United States v. Morison, 844 F.2d 1057, 1071 ("An act is done willfully if it is done voluntarily and intentionally and with the specific intent to do something that the law forbids. That is to say, with a bad purpose either to disobey or to disregard the law."). If any of the disclosed material involves communications intelligence as described in 18 U.S.C. §798, the conduct must be undertaken knowingly and willfully to meet the intent threshold.

[100] See New York Times Co. v. United States, 403 U.S. 713, 721-22 (1971) (Douglas, J., concurring) (rejecting government argument that term "communicate" should be read to include "publish," based on conspicuous absence of the term "publish" in that section of the

Espionage Act and legislative history demonstrating Congress had rejected an effort to reach publication).

[101] See Harold Edgar and Benno C. Schmidt, Jr., Curtiss-Wright Comes Home: Executive Power and National Security Secrecy, 21 HARV. C.R.-C.L. L. REV. 349, 395 (1986) (questioning whether Espionage Act can be construed to except publication).

[102] The data released by WikiLeaks contains some names of Afghans who assisted Coalition Forces, leading to some concern that the Taliban might use the information to seek out those individuals for retaliation. See Eric Schmitt and David E. Sanger, Gates Cites Peril in Leak of Afghan War Logs, N.Y. TIMES, August 2, 2010, at 4. The New York Times, The Guardian, and Der Spiegel published excerpts of the database, but did not publish the names of individual Afghans. Id. No deaths have yet been tied to the leaks. See Robert Burns, Pentagon Sees Deadly Risk in Wikileaks Disclosures, AP NEWSWIRE, August 17, 2010. There appears to be no court precedent interpreting "agent of the United States" in the context of18 U.S.C. §794(a).

[103] See United States v. Zehe, 601 F. Supp. 196, 198 (D.C. Mass. 1985)(citing former 18 U.S.C. §791 repealed by P.L. 87-369, 75 Stat. 795(1961)).

[104] See 70 AM. JUR. 2D Sedition, Subversive Activities and Treason §15 (2005). Courts have not been persuaded that the Treason Clause of the Constitution requires the safeguards associated with treason apply also to similar crimes such as espionage or levying war against the United States. See id.; United States v. Rosenberg, 195 F.2d 583 (2d. Cir.), cert. denied, 344 U.S. 838 (1952)(espionage); United States v. Rodriguez, 803 F.2d 318 (7th Cir.), cert. denied, 480 U.S. 908 (1986) (levying war).

[105] Zehe at 198 ("Espionage against the United States, because it is a crime that by definition threatens this country's security, can therefore be punished by Congress even if committed by a noncitizen outside the United States.").

[106] Id. at 199.

[107] Id.

[108] Henry Giniger and Milt Freudenheim, Free to Spy Another Day?, NY TIMES, Jun 16, 1985, at A.4.

[109] See United States v. Rosen, 445 F. Supp. 2d 602 (E.D. Va. 2006); Jerry Markon, U.S. Drops Case Against Ex-Lobbyists, WASH. POST, May 2, 2009, at A1 (stating the case is the first prosecution under the Espionage Act against civilians not employed by the government).

[110] See William E. Lee, Deep Background: Journalists, Sources, and the Perils of Leaking, 57 AM. U. L. REV. 1453, 1519 (2007) (opining that "the conspiracy charge especially threatens reporter-source transactions where the reporter promises not to disclose the identity of the source").

[111] Time to Call It Quits, WASH. POST, March 11, 2009 (editorial urging Attorney General to drop charges).

[112] See William E. Lee, Probing Secrets: The Press and Inchoate Liability for Newsgathering Crimes, 36 AM. J. CRIM. L. 129, 132-34 (2009). The solicitation theory relied on a 2008 Supreme Court case finding that solicitation of an illegal transaction is not speech deserving of First Amendment protection. United States v. Williams, 553 U.S. 285 (2008). See id. at 133 (citing Brief of the United States at 43-44, United States v. Rosen, 557 F.3d 192 (4th Cir. 2008) (No. 08-4358)). Williams had to do with solicitation of child pornography, but Justice Scalia posed as a rhetorical question whether Congress could criminalize solicitation of information thought to be covered by the Espionage Act: "Is Congress prohibited from punishing those who attempt to acquire what they believe to be national-security documents, but which are actually fakes? To ask is to answer." Williams at 304.

[113] See Markon, supra footnote 109 (quoting Dana J. Boente, the acting U.S. attorney in Alexandria, VA, where the trial was scheduled to take place). The judge found the scienter requirement of 18 U.S.C. §793 to require that the defendants must have reason to believe the communication of the information at issue "could be used to the injury of the United States or to the advantage of any foreign nation." 445 F. Supp. 2d at 639. Moreover, the judge limited the definition of "information related to the national defense" to information that is "potentially damaging to the United States or ... useful to an enemy of the United States." Id. (citing United States v. Morison, 844 F.2d 1057, 1084 (4th Cir. 1988) (Wilkinson, J., concurring)).

[114] United States v. Rosen, 445 F. Supp. 2d 602, 625 (E.D. Va. 2006).

[115] See United States v. Drake, 818 F. Supp. 2d 909, 916 (D. Md. 2011) (distinguishing intent requirements between disclosures involving tangible documents and those involving intangible information); United States v. Kiriakou, 2012 WL 4903319 at *3-5 (E.D. Va. October 16, 2012) (surveying case law and noting that 4th Cir. interlocutory appeal in the Rosen case cast doubt on the district judge's interpretation).

[116] This section is contributed by Michael John Garcia, Legislative Attorney.

[117] For a discussion of these issues as they relate to the possible extradition of Edward Snowden, see CRS Report WSLG561, U.S. May Face Significant Obstacles in Attempt to Apprehend Edward Snowden, by Michael John Garcia.

[118] A current list of countries with which the United States has an extradition treaty is found in CRS Report 98-958, Extradition To and From the United States: Overview of the Law and Recent Treaties, by Michael John Garcia and Charles Doyle, at Appendix A.

[119] See, e.g., Australian Extradition Treaty, art. VII(1), entered into force May 8, 1976, 27 U.S.T. 957 ("Extradition shall not be granted ... when the offense in respect of which extradition is requested is of a political character, or the person whose extradition is requested proves that the extradition request has been made for the purpose of trying or punishing him for an offense of a political character."); Ecuadorian Extradition Treaty, art. 3, entered into force November 12, 1872, 18 Stat. 199 (similar); Norwegian Extradition Treaty, art. 7, entered into force March 7, 1980, 31 U.S.T. 5619 (similar); United Kingdom Extradition Treaty, art. 4, entered into force April 26, 2007, S. TREATY DOC. 108-23 ("Extradition shall not be granted if the offense for which extradition is requested is a political offense."); Swedish Extradition Treaty, art. 5, entered into force December 3, 1963, 14 U.S.T. 1845 ("Extradition shall not be granted....[i]f the offense is regarded by the requested State as a political offense or as an offense connected with a political offense.").

[120] Quinn v. Robinson, 783 F.2d 776, 791 (9th Cir. 1986). See also M. CHERIF BASSIOUNI, INTERNATIONAL EXTRADITION: UNITED STATES LAW AND PRACTICE (BASSIOUNI) 604 (5th ed. 2007).604; Charles Cantrell, The Political Offense Exception to Extradition: A Comparison of the United States, Great Britain and the Republic of Ireland, 60 MARQ. L. REV. 777, 780 (1977).

[121] Quinn, 783 F.2d at 791 (internal citations omitted).

[122] See, e.g., Quinn, 783 F.2d at 791 (citing treason, sedition, and espionage as examples of purely political offenses); BASSIOUNI, supra footnote 120, at 604.

[123] It might be argued that certain offenses punishable under the Espionage Act do not fall under the traditional conception of "espionage," and should therefore not be deemed to be pure political offenses per se. See generally PIETRO VERRI, DICTIONARY OF THE INTERNATIONAL LAW OF ARMED CONFLICT 47 (1992) (espionage is "commonly applied to the efforts made in territory under enemy control by a party to the conflict to collect all information on the enemy that may be useful to the conduct of the war in general

and to that of hostilities in particular....The word espionage is also applied to the collection by States, in peacetime as well as in time of war, of political and military information regarding each other."); Lt. Col. Geoffrey B. Demarest, Espionage in International Law, 24 DENV. J. INT'L L. & POL'Y 321, 324 (1996) ("Throughout history, the terms 'espionage' and 'spying' have carried varying amounts of pejorative baggage. Therefore, any attempt at a precise definition is difficult."). Nonetheless, such an offense might still be deemed to be sufficiently related to political action or informed by political motivations so as to fall under the political offense exception.

[124] Under the doctrine of specialty, sometimes called specialty, "a person who has been brought within the jurisdiction of the court by virtue of proceedings under an extradition treaty, can only be tried for one of the offences described in that treaty, and for the offence with which he is charged in the proceedings for his extradition, until a reasonable time and opportunity have been given him after his release or trial upon such charge, to return to the country from whose asylum he had been forcibly taken under those proceedings." United States v. Alvarez-Machain, 504 U.S. 655, 661 (1992) (quoting United States v. Rauscher, 119 U.S. 407, 430 (1886)). This limitation is expressly included in many treaties.

[125] 18 U.S.C. §641.

[126] E.g., Ecuadorian Extradition Treaty, art. 2, entered into force November 12, 1872, 18 Stat. 199, as modified by supplementary agreement, entered into force May 29, 1941, 55 Stat. 1196 (authorizing extradition for specific offenses).

[127] E.g., Extradition Agreement with the European Union, art. 4(1), entered into force February 1, 2010, S. TREATY DOC. 109-14 (applying in place of any provision in an earlier extradition agreement between the United States and an EU Member State which only authorized extradition only an exclusive list of offenses, and instead providing that "An offense shall be an extraditable offense if it is punishable under the laws of the requesting and requested States by deprivation of liberty for a maximum period of more than one year or by a more severe penalty"); Protocol to Australian Extradition Treaty, art. 1, entered into force December 21, 1992, S. TREATY DOC. 102-23 (replacing provision of earlier extradition agreement listing specific offenses where extradition was available with a provision requiring dual criminality).

[128] It should be noted, however, that extradition treaties may cover certain offenses that can constitute elements of the crime of espionage (e.g., knowingly receiving or fraudulently obtaining property). See, e.g., Extradition Treaty with Belize, appendix listing extraditable offenses, entered into force March 27, 2001, S. TREATY DOC. 106-38.

[129] See CRS Report 94-166, Extraterritorial Application of American Criminal Law, by Charles Doyle.

[130] See CRS Report 98-958, Extradition To and From the United States: Overview of the Law and Recent Treaties, by Michael John Garcia and Charles Doyle. Even among countries holding fairly expansive views of the extraterritorial jurisdiction, there may be substantial differences between the perceptions of common law countries and those of civil law countries, Charles L. Blakesley, A Conceptual Framework for Extradition and Jurisdiction Over Extraterritorial Crimes, 1984 UTAH L. REV. 685 (1984).

[131] IV Michael Abbell & Bruno A. Ristau, International Judicial Assistance: Criminal 64-7 (1990). See, e.g., Ecuadorian Extradition Treaty, art. 1, entered into force November 12, 1872, 18 Stat. 199 (applying to offenses "committed within the jurisdiction of one of the contracting parties").

[132] For examples of specific treaties, see CRS Report 98-958, Extradition To and From the United States: Overview of the Law and Recent Treaties.

[133] BASSIOUNI, supra footnote 120, at 739.

[134] Extradition Agreement with the European Union, art. 10, entered into force February 1, 2010, S. TREATY DOC. 109- 14 (describing factors to be considered by requested state when considering competing extradition requests from the United States or other EU Member States); Bolivian Extradition Treaty, art. X, entered into force November 21, 1996, S. TREATY DOC. 104-22.

[135] See, e.g., Swedish Extradition Treaty, art. IX, entered into force December 3, 1963, 14 U.S.T. 1845 ("A person extradited by virtue of this Convention may not be tried or punished by the requesting State for any offense committed prior to his extradition, other than that which gave rise to the request, nor may he be re-extradited by the requesting State to a third country which claims him, unless the surrendering State so agrees or unless the person extradited, having been set at liberty within the requesting State, remains voluntarily in the requesting State for more than 45 days from the date on which he was released. Upon such release, he shall be informed of the consequences to which his stay in the territory of the requesting State might subject him."); Turkish Extradition Treaty, art. 17, entered into force January 1, 1987, 32 UST 2111 (similar). See also Council of Europe, Convention on Extradition, art. 15, done December 13, 1957 (providing similar requirements for re-extradition among member States of the Council of Europe), available at http://conventions.coe.int/Treaty/EN/Treaties/Html/024.htm.

[136] For an analysis of exceptions to the First Amendment, see CRS Report 95-815, Freedom of Speech and Press: Exceptions to the First Amendment, by Kathleen Ann Ruane.

[137] Sable Communications of California v. Federal Communications Commission, 492 U.S. 115, 126 (1989).

[138] Id.

[139] See Haig v. Agee, 453 U.S. 280 (1981) ("It is 'obvious and unarguable' that no governmental interest is more compelling than the security of the Nation.")(citing Aptheker v. Secretary of State, 378 U.S. 500, 509; accord Cole v. Young, 351 U.S. 536, 546 (1956)).

[140] See Schenck v. United States, 249 U.S. 47 (1919) (formulating "clear and present danger" test).

[141] Brandenburg v. Ohio, 395 U.S. 444 (1969).

[142] Near v. Minnesota, 283 U.S. 697, 716 (1931) ("No one would question but that a government might prevent actual obstruction to its recruiting service or the publication of the sailing dates of transports or the number and location of troops.").

[143] "National Security" is defined as national defense and foreign relations. See Exec. Order No. 13526, 75 Fed. Reg. 707 §6.1(cc) (January 5, 2010).

[144] See, e.g., New York Times Co. v. United States, 403 U.S. 713, 725 (1971) (Brennan, J., concurring) (rejecting as insufficient government's assertions that publication of Pentagon Papers "could," "might," or "may" prejudice the national interest); Elrod v. Burns, 427 U.S. 347, 362 (1976) ("The interest advanced must be paramount, one of vital importance, and the burden is on the government to show the existence of such an interest.") (citing Buckley v. Valeo, 424 U.S. 1, 94(1976); Williams v. Rhodes, 393 U.S. 23, 31-33(1968); NAACP v. Button, 371 U.S. 38, 45 (1963); Bates v. Little Rock, 361 U.S. 516, 524 (1960); NAACP v. Alabama, 357 U.S. 449, 464-466 (1958); Thomas v. Collins, 323 U.S. 516, 530 (1945)).

[145] Bartnicki v. Vopper, 532 U.S. 514, 527 (2001) (citing Smith v. Daily Mail Publishing Co., 443 U.S. 97 (1979)).

[146] Mills v. Alabama, 384 U.S. 214, 218 (1966). Because of the First Amendment purpose to protect the public's ability to discuss governmental affairs along with court decisions denying that it provides any special rights to journalists, e.g., Branzburg v. Hayes, 408 U.S.

665 (1972), it is not likely a plausible argument to posit that it does not apply to the foreign press. See United States v. 18 Packages of Magazines 238 F. Supp. 846, 847-848 (D.C. Cal. 1964) ("Even if it be conceded, arguendo, that the 'foreign press' is not a direct beneficiary of the Amendment, the concession gains nought for the Government in this case. The First Amendment does protect the public of this country. ... The First Amendment surely was designed to protect the rights of readers and distributors of publications no less than those of writers or printers. Indeed, the essence of the First Amendment right to freedom of the press is not so much the right to print as it is the right to read. The rights of readers are not to be curtailed because of the geographical origin of printed materials."). The Supreme Court invalidated, on First Amendment grounds, a statute that required postal authorities to detain unsealed mail from abroad deemed to contain "communist political propaganda" unless the recipient affirms a desire to receive it. Lamont v. Postmaster General, 381 U.S. 301 (1965). Likewise, the fact that WikiLeaks is not a typical newsgathering and publishing organization would likely make little difference under First Amendment analysis. The Supreme Court has not established clear boundaries between the protection of speech and that of the press, nor has it sought to develop criteria for identifying what constitutes "the press" that might qualify its members for privileges not available to anyone else. See generally CONGRESSIONAL RESEARCH SERVICE, THE CONSTITUTION OF THE UNITED STATES: ANALYSIS AND INTERPRETATION, SEN. DOC. NO. 108- 17, at 1083-86 (2002), available at http://crs.gov/conan/default.aspx?mode=topic&doc= Amendment 01.xml&t=2|3.

[147] Exec. Order No. 13526, 75 Fed. Reg. 707 §1.2 (January 5, 2010) ("Classified National Security Information"). Section 1.3 defines three levels of classification:

"Top Secret" shall be applied to information, the unauthorized disclosure of which reasonably could be expected to cause exceptionally grave damage to the national security that the original classification authority is able to identify or describe.

"Secret" shall be applied to information, the unauthorized disclosure of which reasonably could be expected to cause serious damage to the national security that the original classification authority is able to identify or describe.

"Confidential" shall be applied to information, the unauthorized disclosure of which reasonably could be expected to cause damage to the national security that the original classification authority is able to identify or describe.

[148] United States v. Heine, 151 F.2d 813 (2d Cir.1945) (information must be "closely held" to be considered "related to the national defense" within the meaning of the espionage statutes).

[149] See, e.g., United States v. Abu-Jihaad 600 F.Supp.2d 362, 385-86 (D. Conn. 2009) (although completely inaccurate information might not be covered, information related to the scheduled movements of naval vessels was sufficient to bring materials within the ambit of national defense information).

[150] See, e.g., Haig v. Agee, 453 U.S. 280, 291 (1981) ("Matters intimately related to foreign policy and national security are rarely proper subjects for judicial intervention.").

[151] See, e.g., United States v. Morison, 844 F.2d 1057, 1086 (4th Cir. 1988) (Phillips, J., concurring) ("... I assume we reaffirm today, that notwithstanding information may have been classified, the government must still be required to prove that it was in fact 'potentially damaging ... or useful,' i.e., that the fact of classification is merely probative, not conclusive, on that issue, though it must be conclusive on the question of authority to possess or receive the information. This must be so to avoid converting the Espionage Act into the simple Government Secrets Act which Congress has refused to enact.") (emphasis in original).

[152] See, e.g., Scarbeck v. United States, 317 F.2d 546 (D.C. Cir. 1962) (holding government did not have to show documents were properly classified "as affecting the national defense" to convict employee under 50 U.S.C. §783, which prohibits government employees from transmitting classified documents to foreign agents or entities).

[153] See United States v. Dedeyan, 594 F.2d 36, 39 (4th Cir. 1978).

[154] 312 U.S. 19 (1941).

[155] Id. at 28.

[156] Id. at 32. The information defendant was charged with passing to the Soviet government had to do with U.S. intelligence on the activities of Japanese citizens in the United States.

[157] Id. at 31.

[158] 844 F.2d 1057 (4th Cir.), cert. denied, 488 U.S. 908 (1988).

[159] Efforts to prosecute Daniel Ellsberg and Anthony Russo in connection with the disclosure of the Pentagon Papers were unsuccessful after the judge dismissed them for prosecutorial misconduct. More recently, a Defense Department employee pleaded guilty to charges under the Espionage Act for disclosing classified material to lobbyists and to journalists. United States v. Franklin, Cr. No. 05-225 (E.D. Va., 2005). For a description of these and other relevant cases, see Lee, supra footnote 110.

[160] But see Scarbeck v. United States, 317 F.2d 546 (D.C. Cir. 1962) (holding that government did not need to prove proper classification of documents to prove a violation).

[161] 844 F.2d at 1073-74. Morison had stated that he sought the publication of the photos because they would demonstrate to the public the gravity of the threat posed by the Soviet Union, which he hoped would result in an increased defense budget. See P. Weiss, The Quiet Coup: U.S. v. Morison - A Victory for Secret Government, HARPER'S, September 1989.

[162] See Jack Nelson, U.S. Government Secrecy and the Current Crackdown on Leaks 8, The Joan Shorenstein Center on the Press, Politics and Public Policy, Working Paper Series 2003-1 (2002), available at http://www.hks.harvard.edu/ presspol/publications/ papers/working_ papers/2003_01_nelson.pdf.

[163] Valerie Strauss, Navy Analyst Morison Receives a Pardon, WASH. POST, January 21, 2001, at A17. Senator Daniel Patrick Moynihan wrote a letter in support of Morison's pardon and explaining his view that "An evenhanded prosecution of leakers could imperil an entire administration," and that "[i]f ever there were to be widespread action taken, it would significantly hamper the ability of the press to function." Letter, Sen. Daniel Patrick Moynihan to President Clinton, September 29, 1998, available at http://www.fas.org/sgp/ news/2001/04/moynihan.html.

[164] New York Times Co. v. United States, 403 U.S. 713 (1971) (per curiam).

[165] Nebraska Press Association v. Stuart, 427 U.S. 539, 559 (1976) (striking down a court order restraining the publication or broadcast of accounts of confessions or admissions made by the defendant at a criminal trial).

[166] 403 U.S. at 734-40 (White, J. with Stewart, J. concurring); id. at 745-47 (Marshall, J., concurring); id. at 752 (Burger, C.J., dissenting); id. at 752-59 (Harlan, J., joined by Burger, C.J. and Blackmun, J., dissenting). See David Topol, Note, United States v. Morison: A Threat to the First Amendment Right to Publish Security Information, 43 S.C. L. REV. 581, 586 (noting that three concurring Justices suggested that the government could convict the newspapers under the Espionage Act even though it could not enjoin them from printing the documents, while the three dissenting Justices thought the injunction should issue).

[167] Smith v. Daily Mail Publishing Co., 443 U.S. 97, 102-03 (1979) ("Whether we view the statute as a prior restraint or as a penal sanction for publishing lawfully obtained, truthful information is not dispositive because even the latter action requires the highest form of

state interest to sustain its validity.") The case involved the prosecution of a newspaper for publishing the name of a juvenile defendant without court permission, in violation of state law.

[168] For a list of the types of damage the government argued would ensue if its efforts to enjoin publication failed, see William H. Freivogel, Publishing National Security Secrets: The Case for "Benign Indeterminacy," 3 J. NAT'L SECURITY L. & POL'Y 95, 112-13 (2009).

[169] See, e.g., Landmark Commc'ns. v. Virginia, 435 U.S. 829, 837 (1978).

[170] Florida Star v. B.J.F. 491 U.S. 524, 535 (1989). The Court also questioned whether the receipt of information can ever constitutionally be proscribed. Id. at 536.

[171] Daily Mail, 443 U.S at 103. Here, routine newsgathering consisted of perusing publicly available court records.

[172] 532 U.S. 514 (2001).

[173] See Boehner v. McDermott, 484 F.3d 573 (D.C. Cir. 2007) (en banc) (Congressman, bound by Ethics Committee rules not to disclose certain information, had no First Amendment right to disclose to press contents of tape recording illegally made by third party).

[174] 18 U.S.C. §793(c). The provision does not appear to cover receipt of intangible information.

[175] See, e.g., The Espionage Act and the Legal and Constitutional Issues Raised by WikiLeaks, Hearing before the H. Comm. on the Judiciary, 111th Cong. (2010).

[176] See id.

[177] H.R. 4392, 106th Cong. §304 (enrolled bill); H.R. 2943, 107th Cong; Previous unsuccessful bills to criminalize leaks of classified information by government officers and employees include H.R. 319, 104th Cong. (providing for prison term up to 20 years as well as possible fine); H.R. 271, 103d Cong. (same); H.R. 363, 102d Cong. (same); H.R. 279, 101st Cong.; H.R. 3066, 100th Cong.; H.R. 3468, 96th Cong (would have excluded non-government employees from accomplice liability); H.R. 6057, 95th Cong.; H.R. 13602, 94th Cong.

[178] 18 U.S.C. §1924 prohibits removal of government-owned or controlled classified information by a government employee without authorization. 50 U.S.C. §783 covers only information classified by the President or an executive agency transmitted by a government employee to a foreign government. 18 U.S.C. §§793 and 794 are potentially broader than these in that they cover information "related to the national defense," by government employees and others without regard to the identity of the recipient of the information, but these require intent or knowledge regarding harm to the national defense.

[179] "Classified information" was defined in the proposed measure to mean "information or material designated and clearly marked or represented, or that the person knows or has reason to believe has been determined by appropriate authorities, pursuant to the provisions of a statute or Executive Order, as requiring protection against unauthorized disclosure for reasons of national security."

[180] See H.Rept. 106-969 at 44 (2000).

[181] H.R. 4392 §304, 106th Congress.

[182] Message on Returning Without Approval to the House of Representatives the "Intelligence Authorization Act for Fiscal Year 2001", 36 WEEKLY COMP. PRES. DOC. 278 (November 4, 2000).

[183] Id.

[184] The Classified Information Protection Act of 2001, H.R. 2943, 107th Cong.

[185] Intelligence Authorization Act for Fiscal Year 2002, P.L. 107-108, §310 (2001).

[186] S. 3774, 109th Cong.

[187] Report to Congress on Unauthorized Disclosure of Classified Information, October 15, 2002 (citations omitted).

[188] The bill was introduced at the end of the 111th Congress as S. 4004.

[189] A substantially identical bill was introduced as H.R. 6506 at the end of the 111th Congress.

[190] See also S. 4051 (111th Cong.) (identical to more recent version except that it included jurisdiction over aiders and abettors of violations of the provision enforcing secrecy obligations, at least where such violations occurred overseas).

[191] The courts have permitted government agencies to enjoin their employees and former employees from publishing information they learned on the job, United States v. Marchetti, 466 F.2d 1309 (4th Cir.), cert. denied, 409 U.S. 1063 (1972), and permitted harsh sanctions against employees who publish even unclassified information in violation of an obligation to obtain prepublication clearance, Snepp v. United States, 444 U.S. 507 (1980).

In: NSA Intelligence Collection, Leaks … ISBN: 978-1-62948-937-7
Editor: Simon Cepeda

Chapter 4

THE PROTECTION OF CLASSIFIED INFORMATION: THE LEGAL FRAMEWORK*

Jennifer K. Elsea

SUMMARY

This report provides an overview of the relationship between executive and legislative authority over national security information, and summarizes the current laws that form the legal framework protecting classified information, including current executive orders and some agency regulations pertaining to the handling of unauthorized disclosures of classified information by government officers and employees. The report also summarizes criminal laws that pertain specifically to the unauthorized disclosure of classified information, as well as civil and administrative penalties. Finally, the report describes some recent developments in executive branch security policies and relevant legislative activity.

* This is an edited, reformatted and augmented version of a Congressional Research Service publication, CRS Report for Congress RS21900, from www.crs.gov, prepared for Members and Committees of Congress, dated January 10, 2013.

BACKGROUND

Prior to the New Deal, classification decisions were left to military regulation.[1] In 1940, President Franklin Roosevelt issued an executive order authorizing government officials to protect information pertaining to military and naval installations.[2] Presidents since that time have continued to set the federal government's classification standards by executive order, but with one critical difference: while President Roosevelt cited specific statutory authority for his action, later Presidents have cited general statutory *and constitutional* authority.[3]

The Supreme Court has never directly addressed the extent to which Congress may constrain the executive branch's power in this area. Citing the President's constitutional role as Commander-inChief,[4] the Supreme Court has repeatedly stated in dicta that "[the President's] authority to classify and control access to information bearing on national security ... flows primarily from this Constitutional investment of power in the President and exists quite apart from any explicit congressional grant."[5] This language has been interpreted by some to indicate that the President has virtually plenary authority to control classified information. On the other hand, the Supreme Court has suggested that "Congress could certainly [provide] that the Executive Branch adopt new [classification procedures] or [establish] its own procedures—subject only to whatever limitations the Executive Privilege may be held to impose on such congressional ordering."[6] In fact, Congress established a separate regime in the Atomic Energy Act for the protection of nuclear-related "Restricted Data."[7]

Congress has directed the President to establish procedures governing the access to classified material so that no person can gain such access without having undergone a background check.[8]

Congress also directed the President, in formulating the classification procedures, to adhere to certain minimum standards of due process with regard to access to classified information.[9] These include the establishment of uniform procedures for, *inter alia*, background checks, denial of access to classified information, and notice of such denial.[10] The statute also explicitly states that the agency heads are not required to comply with the due process requirement in denying or revoking an employee's security clearance where doing so could damage national security, although the statute directs agency heads to submit a report to the congressional intelligence committees in such a case.[11]

With the authority to determine classification standards vested in the President, these standards tend to change whenever a new administration takes control of the White House.[12] The differences between the standards of one administration and the next have often been dramatic. As one congressionally authorized commission put it in 1997:

> The rules governing how best to protect the nation's secrets, while still insuring that the American public has access to information on the operations of its government, past and present, have shifted along with the political changes in Washington. Over the last fifty years, with the exception of the Kennedy Administration, a new executive order on classification was issued each time one of the political parties regained control of the Executive Branch. These have often been at variance with one another ... at times even reversing outright the policies of the previous order.[13]

Various congressional committees have investigated ways to bring some continuity to the classification system and to limit the President's broad powers to shield information from public examination.[14] In 1966, Congress passed the Freedom of Information Act (FOIA), creating a presumption that government information will be open to the public unless it falls into one of FOIA's exceptions. One exception covers information that, under executive order, must be kept secret for national security or foreign policy reasons.[15] In 2000, Congress enacted the Public Interest Declassification Act of 2000,[16] which established the Public Interest Declassification Board to advise the President on matters regarding the declassification of certain information, but the act expressly disclaims any intent to restrict agency heads from classifying or continuing the classification of information under their purview, nor does it create any rights or remedies that may be enforced in court.[17] Most recently, Congress passed the Reducing Over-Classification Act, P.L. 111-258, which, among other things, requires executive branch agencies' inspectors general to conduct assessments of their agencies' implementation of classification policies.[18]

EXECUTIVE ORDER 13526

The present standards for classifying and declassifying information were last amended on December 29, 2009.[19] Under these standards, the President, Vice President, agency heads, and any other officials designated by the

President may classify information upon a determination that the unauthorized disclosure of such information could reasonably be expected to damage national security.[20] Such information must be owned by, produced by, or under the control of the federal government, and must concern one of the following:

- military plans, weapons systems, or operations;
- foreign government information;
- intelligence activities, intelligence sources/methods, cryptology;
- foreign relations or foreign activities of the United States, including confidential sources;
- scientific, technological, or economic matters relating to national security;
- federal programs for safeguarding nuclear materials or facilities;
- vulnerabilities or capabilities of national security systems; or
- weapons of mass destruction.[21]

Information may be classified at one of three levels based on the amount of danger that its unauthorized disclosure could reasonably be expected to cause to national security.[22] Information is classified as "Top Secret" if its unauthorized disclosure could reasonably be expected to cause "exceptionally grave damage" to national security. The standard for "Secret" information is "serious damage" to national security, while for "confidential" information the standard is "damage" to national security. Significantly, for each level, the original classifying officer must identify or describe the specific danger potentially presented by the information's disclosure.[23] In case of significant doubt as to the need to classify information or the level of classification appropriate, the information is to remain unclassified or be classified at the lowest level of protection considered appropriate.[24]

The officer who originally classifies the information establishes a date for declassification based upon the expected duration of the information's sensitivity. If the office cannot set an earlier declassification date, then the information must be marked for declassification in 10 years' time or 25 years, depending on the sensitivity of the information.[25] The deadline for declassification can be extended if the threat to national security still exists.[26]

Classified information is required to be declassified "as soon as it no longer meets the standards for classification."[27] The original classifying agency has the authority to declassify information when the public interest in disclosure outweighs the need to protect that information.[28] On December 31,

2006, and every year thereafter, all information that has been classified for 25 years or longer and has been determined to have "permanent historical value" under Title 44 of the U.S. Code will be automatically declassified, although agency heads can exempt from this requirement classified information that continues to be sensitive in a variety of specific areas.[29]

Agencies are required to review classification determinations upon a request for such a review that specifically identifies the materials so that the agency can locate them, unless the materials identified are part of an operational file exempt under the Freedom of Information Act (FOIA)[30] or are the subject of pending litigation.[31] This requirement does not apply to information that has undergone declassification review in the previous two years; information that is exempted from review under the National Security Act;[32] or information classified by the incumbent President and staff, the Vice President and staff (in the performance of executive duties), commissions appointed by the President, or other entities within the executive office of the President that advise the President.[33] Each agency that has classified information is required to establish a system for periodic declassification reviews.[34] The National Archivist is required to establish a similar systemic review of classified information that has been transferred to the National Archives.[35]

Access to classified information is generally limited to those who demonstrate their eligibility to the relevant agency head, sign a nondisclosure agreement, and have a need to know the information.[36] The need-to-know requirement can be waived, however, for former Presidents and Vice Presidents, historical researchers, and former policy-making officials who were appointed by the President or Vice President.[37] The information being accessed may not be removed from the controlling agency's premises without permission. Each agency is required to establish systems for controlling the distribution of classified information.[38]

The Information Security Oversight Office (ISOO)—an office within the National Archives—is charged with overseeing compliance with the classification standards and promulgating directives to that end.[39] ISOO is headed by a Director, who is appointed by the Archivist of the United States, and who has the authority to order declassification of information that, in the Director's view, is classified in violation of the aforementioned classification standards.[40] In addition, there is an Interagency Security Classifications Appeals Panel ("the Panel"), headed by the ISOO Director and made up of representatives of the heads of various agencies, including the Departments of Defense, Justice, and State, as well as the Central Intelligence Agency, and the

National Archives.[41] The Panel is empowered to decide appeals of classifications challenges[42] and to review automatic and mandatory declassifications.

If the ISOO Director finds a violation of E.O. 13526 or its implementing directives, then the Director must notify the appropriate classifying agency so that corrective steps can be taken.

HANDLING OF UNAUTHORIZED DISCLOSURES

Under E.O. 13526, each respective agency is responsible for maintaining control over classified information it originates and is responsible for establishing uniform procedures to protect classified information and automated information systems in which classified information is stored or transmitted.

Standards for safeguarding classified information, including the handling, storage, distribution, transmittal, and destruction of and accounting for classified information, are developed by the ISOO. Agencies that receive information classified elsewhere are not permitted to transfer the information further without approval from the classifying agency. Persons authorized to disseminate classified information outside the executive branch are required to ensure it receives protection equivalent to those required internally. In the event of a knowing, willful, or negligent unauthorized disclosure (or any such action that could reasonably be expected to result in an unauthorized disclosure), the agency head or senior agency official is required to notify ISOO and to "take appropriate and prompt corrective action." Officers and employees of the United States (including contractors, licensees, etc.) who commit a violation are subject to sanctions that can range from reprimand to termination.[43]

Executive Order 12333, United States Intelligence Activities,[44] spells out the responsibilities of members of the Intelligence Community[45] for the protection of intelligence information, including intelligence sources and methods. Under Section 1.7 of E.O. 12333, heads of departments and agencies with organizations in the Intelligence Community (or the heads of such organizations, if appropriate) must report possible violations of federal criminal laws to the Attorney General "in a manner consistent with the protection of intelligence sources and methods."

Information Security Oversight Office

ISOO Directive No. 1 (32 CFR Part 2001) provides further direction for agencies with responsibilities for safeguarding classified information. Section 2001.41 states:

> Authorized persons who have access to classified information are responsible for: (a) Protecting it from persons without authorized access to that information, to include securing it in approved equipment or facilities whenever it is not under the direct control of an authorized person; (b) Meeting safeguarding requirements prescribed by the agency head; and (c) Ensuring that classified information is not communicated over unsecured voice or data circuits, in public conveyances or places, or in any other manner that permits interception by unauthorized persons.

Section 2001.45 of ISOO Directive No. 1 requires agency heads to establish a system of appropriate control measures to limit access to classified information to authorized persons. Section 2001.46 requires that classified information is transmitted and received in an authorized manner that facilitates detection of tampering and precludes inadvertent access. Persons who transmit classified information are responsible for ensuring that the intended recipients are authorized to receive classified information and have the capacity to store classified information appropriately. Documents classified "Top Secret" that are physically transmitted outside secure facilities must be properly marked and wrapped in two layers to conceal the contents, and must remain under the constant and continuous protection of an authorized courier. In addition to the methods prescribed for the outside transmittal of Top Secret documents, documents classified at Secret or Confidential levels may be mailed in accordance with the prescribed procedures.

Agency heads are required to establish procedures for receiving classified information in a manner that precludes unauthorized access, provides for detection of tampering and confirmation of contents, and ensures the timely acknowledgment of the receipt (in the case of Top Secret and Secret information).

Section 2001.48 prescribes measures to be taken in the event of loss, possible compromise, or unauthorized disclosure. It states: "Any person who has knowledge that classified information has been or may have been lost, possibly compromised or disclosed to an unauthorized person(s) shall immediately report the circumstances to an official designated for this purpose."

Agency heads are required to establish appropriate procedures to conduct an inquiry or investigation into the loss, possible compromise or unauthorized disclosure of classified information, in order to implement "appropriate corrective actions" and to "ascertain the degree of damage to national security."

The department or agency in which the compromise occurred must also advise any other government agency or foreign government agency whose interests are involved of the circumstances and findings that affect their information or interests.

Agency heads are to establish procedures to ensure coordination with legal counsel in any case where a formal disciplinary action beyond a reprimand is contemplated against a person believed responsible for the unauthorized disclosure of classified information. Whenever a criminal violation appears to have occurred and a criminal prosecution is contemplated, agency heads are to ensure coordination with the Department of Justice and the legal counsel of the agency where the individual believed to be responsible is assigned or employed. Violators are generally subject to imprisonment or fine, and in some cases, loss of retirement or other benefits.

Intelligence Community

The most recent intelligence community directives related to the safeguarding of classified information appear to be Intelligence Community Directive (ICD) 700, Protection of National Intelligence, effective June 7, 2012,[46] and ICD 701, Security Policy Directive for Unauthorized Disclosures of Classified Information, effective March 14, 2007.[47] ICD 700 mandates an integration of counterintelligence and security functions for the purpose of protecting national intelligence and sensitive information and, among other things, to strengthen "deterrence, detection, and mitigation of insider threats, defined as personnel who use their authorized access to do harm to the security of the US through espionage, terrorism, unauthorized disclosure of information, or through the loss or degradation of resources or capabilities."[48] Under ICD 701, Senior Officials of the Intelligence Community (SOICs)[49] are to promptly notify the Director of National Intelligence (DNI) and, if appropriate, law enforcement authorities of any actual or suspected unauthorized disclosure of classified information, including any media leak, that is likely to cause damage to national security interests, unless the disclosure is the subject of a counterespionage or counterintelligence investigation. Disclosures to be reported include:

> Unauthorized disclosure to an international organization, foreign power, agent of a foreign power, or terrorist organization;
> National intelligence activities or information that may be at risk of appearing in the public media, either foreign or domestic, without official authorization;
> Loss or compromise of classified information that poses a risk to human life;
> Loss or compromise of classified information that is indicative of a systemic compromise;
> Loss or compromise of classified information storage media or equipment; Discovery of clandestine surveillance and listening devices;
> Loss or compromise of classified information revealing U.S. or a foreign intelligence partner's intelligence operations or locations, or impairing foreign relations;
> Such other disclosures of classified information that could adversely affect activities related to US national security; and
> Loss or compromise of classified information revealing intelligence sources or methods, US intelligence requirements, capabilities and relationships with the US Government.

Upon determining that a compromise meeting the above reporting criteria has or may have occurred, the SOIC is required promptly to report it to the DNI, through the Special Security Center (SSC), and to any other element with responsibility for the material at issue.

The SOIC is then required to provide updated reports as appropriate (or as directed). This process occurs in tandem with any required reporting to law enforcement authorities.

The required formal notification to the DNI is to include a complete statement of the facts, the scope of the unauthorized disclosure, sources and methods that may be at risk, the potential effect of the disclosure on national security, and corrective or mitigating actions.

SOICs are further required to identify all factors that contributed to the compromise of classified information and take corrective action or make recommendations to the DNI.

Department of Defense

Department of Defense Directive 5210.50, "Unauthorized Disclosure of Classified Information to the Public" (July 22, 2005)[50] governs procedures for handling unauthorized disclosures of classified information to the public. In the event of a known or suspected disclosure of classified information, the heads of DOD components must report the incident to the Deputy Secretary of Defense of Intelligence and conduct a preliminary investigation to confirm that classified information was disclosed, identify the particulars of the incident and who was involved, ascertain whether the information was properly classified or was authorized to be released, and identify any leads that might identify the person or persons responsible. The preliminary investigation should also ascertain whether further inquiry might increase the damage caused by the compromise.

Enclosure 2 to Directive 5210.50 lists factors for determining whether to initiate an additional investigation by military, criminal, or counterintelligence investigative organizations, or the Department of Justice:

> The accuracy of the information disclosed.
>
> The damage to national security caused by the disclosure and whether there were compromises regarding sensitive aspects of current classified projects, intelligence sources, or intelligence methods.
>
> The extent to which the disclosed information was circulated and the number of persons known to have access to it.
>
> The degree to which an investigation shall increase the damage caused by the disclosure. The existence of any investigative leads.
>
> The reasonable expectation of repeated disclosures.
>
> The extent to which the classified information was circulated outside the Department of Defense.

If classified DOD information appears in a newspaper or other media, the head of the appropriate DOD component is responsible for the preparation of a "DOJ Media Leak Questionnaire" to submit to the Deputy Secretary of Defense for Intelligence, who prepares a letter for the Chief, Internal Security Section of the Criminal Division at the Department of Justice. The following eleven questions[51] are to be promptly and fully addressed:

- Date and identity of the article containing classified information.
- Specific statements that are classified, and whether the information is properly classified.

- Whether disclosed information is accurate.
- Whether the information came from a specific document, and if so, the originating office and person responsible for its security.
- Extent of official circulation of the information.
- Whether information has been the subject of prior official release.
- Whether pre-publication clearance was sought.
- Whether sufficient information or background data has been published officially or in the press to make educated speculation on the matter possible.
- Whether information is to be made available for use in a criminal prosecution.
- Whether information has been considered for declassification.
- The effect the disclosure of the classified data might have on the national defense.

PENALTIES FOR UNAUTHORIZED DISCLOSURE

In addition to administrative penalties agencies may employ to enforce information security, there are several statutory provisions that address the protection of classified information as such. No blanket prohibition exists to make it unlawful simply to disclose without authority any information that is classified by the government for national security reasons.[52]

Criminal Penalties

Generally, federal law prescribes a prison sentence of no more than a year and/or a $1,000 fine for officers and employees of the federal government who knowingly remove classified material without the authority to do so and with the intention of keeping that material at an unauthorized location.[53] Stiffer penalties—fines of up to $10,000 and imprisonment for up to 10 years—attach when a federal employee transmits classified information to anyone that the employee has reason to believe is an agent of a foreign government.[54] A fine and a 10-year prison term also await anyone, government employee or not, who publishes, makes available to an unauthorized person, or otherwise uses to the United States' detriment classified information regarding the codes, cryptography, and communications intelligence utilized by the United States or a foreign government.[55] Finally, the disclosure of classified information that discloses any information identifying a covert agent, when done intentionally by a person with authorized access to such identifying information, is punishable by imprisonment for up to 15 years.[56] A similar disclosure by one who learns the identity of a covert agent as a result of having authorized access to classified information is punishable by not more than 10 years' imprisonment. Under the same provision, a person who undertakes a "pattern of activities intended to identify and expose covert agents" with reason to believe such activities would impair U.S. foreign intelligence activities, and who then discloses the identities uncovered as a result is subject to three years' imprisonment, whether or not violator has access to classified information.[57]

Civil Penalties and Other Measures

In addition to the criminal penalties outlined above, the executive branch employs numerous means of deterring unauthorized disclosures by government personnel using administrative measures based on terms of employment contracts. The agency may impose disciplinary action or revoke a person's security clearance. The revocation of a security clearance is usually not reviewable by the Merit System Protection Board[58] and may mean the loss of government employment. Government employees may be subject to monetary penalties for disclosing classified information.[59] Violators of the Espionage Act and the Atomic Energy Act provisions may be subject to loss of their retirement pay.[60]

Agencies also rely on contractual agreements with employees, who typically must sign nondisclosure agreements prior to obtaining access to classified information,[61] sometimes agreeing to submit all materials that the employee desires to publish to a review by the agency. The Supreme Court enforced such a contract against a former employee of the Central Intelligence Agency (CIA), upholding the government's imposition of a constructive trust on the profits of a book the employee sought to publish without first submitting it to CIA for review.[62]

In 1986, the Espionage Act was amended to provide for the forfeiture of any property derived from or used in the commission of an offense.[63] Violators of the Atomic Energy Act may be subjected to a civil penalty of up to $100,000 for each violation of Energy Department regulations regarding dissemination of unclassified information about nuclear facilities.[64]

Under some circumstances, the government can also use injunctions to prevent disclosures of information. The courts have generally upheld injunctions against former employees' publishing information they learned through access to classified information.[65] The Supreme Court also upheld the State Department's revocation of passports for overseas travel by persons planning to expose U.S. covert intelligence agents, despite the fact that the purpose was to disrupt U.S. intelligence activities rather than to assist a foreign government.[66]

DECLASSIFICATION VS. LEAKS AND "INSTANT DECLASSIFICATION"

As noted above, E.O. 13526 sets the official procedures for the declassification of information. Once information is declassified, it may be released to persons without a security clearance.[67] Leaks, by contrast, might be defined as the release of classified information to persons without a security clearance, typically journalists. Recent high-profile leaks of information regarding sensitive covert operations in news stories that seemed to some to portray the Obama Administration in a favorable light[68] raised questions regarding the practice of "instant declassification," or whether disclosure of classified information to journalists may ever be said to be an "authorized disclosure" by a senior official.

The processes for declassification set forth in E.O. 13526 seem to presuppose that agencies and classifying officials will not have any need or desire to disclose classified information in their possession other than to comply with the regulations. Yet it has long been noted that there seems to be an informal process for "instant declassification" of information whose release to the public serves an immediate need. As Representative William Moorhead, at the time chairman of the Foreign Operations and Government Information Subcommittee of the House Government Operations Committee, stated in 1974:

> Critics of the present system of handling classified information within the Executive Branch point to an obvious double standard. On one hand, the full power of the Government's legal system is exercised against certain newspapers for publishing portions of the Pentagon Papers and against someone like Daniel Ellsberg for his alleged role in their being made public. This is contrasted with other actions by top Executive

> officials who utilize the technique of "instant declassification" of information they want leaked. Sometimes it is an "off-the-record" press briefing or "backgrounders" that becomes "on-the-record" at the conclusion of the briefing or at some future politically strategic time. Such Executive Branch leaks may be planted with friendly news columnists. Or, the President himself may exercise his prerogative as Commander in Chief to declassify specific information in an address to the Nation or in a message to the Congress seeking additional funds for a weapons systems.[69]

Nothing in the Executive Order addresses an informal procedure for releasing classified information. E.O. 13526 Section 1.1. provides that "[c]lassified information shall not be declassified automatically as a result of any *unauthorized* disclosure of identical or similar information," but does not address what happens in the event of a disclosure that was in fact authorized. By definition, classified information is designated as such based on whether its *unauthorized* disclosure can reasonably be expected to cause a certain level of damage to national security.[70] This may be read to suggest that disclosures may be authorized under such circumstances when no damage to national security is reasonably expected. Nothing in the order provides explicit authority to release classified information that exists apart from the authority to declassify, but it is possible that such discretionary authority is recognized to release information outside the community of authorized holders without formally declassifying it.

Part 4 of the Executive Order describes safeguarding of classified information from unauthorized disclosure[71] and preventing access to such information by "unauthorized persons." Most of the provisions appear to envision classified documents or communications and storage devices used for classified information rather than the spoken word. Section 4.1(g) requires agency heads and the Director of National Intelligence to "establish controls to ensure that classified information is used, processed, stored, reproduced, transmitted, and destroyed under conditions that provide adequate protection and prevent access by unauthorized persons." If "transmitted" is read to include oral dissemination and "unauthorized persons" is read to mean persons who do not meet the criteria set forth in Section 4.1(a),[72] then it would seem that agency heads who approve leaks could be in breach of their responsibilities under the Order.

Moreover, there is a provision for "emergency disclosure" of classified information "when necessary to respond to an imminent threat to life or in defense of the homeland" to "an individual or individuals who are otherwise not eligible for access." Section 4.2(b) provides that such disclosures must be in accordance with implementing regulations or procedures the classifying agency implements; must be undertaken in such a way as to minimize the information disclosed and the number of individuals who receive it; and must be reported promptly to the originator. Information disclosed under this provision is not deemed to be declassified. The existence of this provision could be read to cut against an interpretation that permits selected release of classified information to reporters for broader dissemination, but it could also be read not to preclude a different procedure by which an agency head who is the original classifying authority for the information at issue might simply authorize remarks to the press that reference classified information in such a way as to minimize harm to national security.

As a practical matter, however, there is little to stop agency heads and other high-ranking officials from releasing classified information to persons without a security clearance when it is seen as suiting government needs. The Attorney General has prosecutorial discretion to choose which leaks to prosecute. If in fact a case can be made that a senior official has made or authorized the disclosure of classified information, successful prosecution under current laws may be impossible because the scienter requirement (i.e., guilty state of mind) is not likely to be met. The Espionage Act of 1917, for example, requires proof that the discloser has the intent or reason to believe the information will be used against the United States or to the benefit of a foreign nation.[73] In cases under the Espionage Act, courts tend to show deference to the government with respect to the sensitivity of whatever classified information was released. Oftentimes in such cases, knowledge that the information is classified is enough to persuade a court that damage to national security can be expected. However, in the event the disclosure was made or authorized by a person who has the authority to make such determinations, it would seem likely that court deference would result in acquittal absent some overwhelming proof of ill intent. A belief on the part of a lower level official that a particular disclosure was authorized could serve as an effective defense to any prosecution, and could entitle the defendant to depose high level government officials in preparation for his or her defense.

Executive branch policy appears to treat an official disclosure as a declassifying event, while non-attributed disclosures have no effect on the classification status of the information. For example, the Department of Defense instructs agency officials, in the event that classified information appears in the media, to neither confirm nor deny the accuracy of the information.[74] The Under Secretary of Defense for Intelligence is then advised to "consult with the Assistant Secretary of Defense for Public Affairs and other officials having a primary interest in the information to determine if the information was officially released under proper authority."[75] The regulation does not clarify what happens in the event the disclosure turns out to have been properly authorized. It appears no further action need be taken, whether to inform employees that the information no longer need be protected or to make annotations in classified records to reflect the newly declassified status of the information. In any event, any documents that contain that information potentially contain other classified information as well, in which case each such document would retain the highest level of classification applicable to information in the document. Thus, it seems unlikely that the authorized disclosure of classified information to the media will often result in the public release of any records.

RECENT DEVELOPMENTS

The following sections address efforts undertaken by the executive branch and Congress to address disclosures of classified information by federal employees.

Executive Branch Initiatives

In October 2011 the President issued Executive Order 13587, "Structural Reforms to Improve the Security of Classified Networks and the Responsible Sharing and Safeguarding of Classified Information."[76] Among other measures, it establishes an interagency Insider Threat Task Force with a mandate to:

> develop a Government-wide program (insider threat program) for deterring, detecting, and mitigating insider threats, including the safeguarding of classified information from exploitation, compromise, or other unauthorized disclosure, taking into account risk levels, as well as the distinct needs, missions, and systems of individual agencies. This program shall include development of policies, objectives, and priorities for establishing and integrating security, counterintelligence, user audits and monitoring, and other safeguarding capabilities and practices within agencies.[77]

The President issued the resulting new policy and minimum standards for agencies in implementing their own insider threat programs in November 2012.[78]

The Director of National Intelligence issued a revised directive in June 2012 to govern the protection of national intelligence by the intelligence community.[79] It emphasizes the integration of security and counterintelligence functions for, among other purposes, strengthening deterrence, detection and mitigation of "insider threats," which it defined as "personnel who use their authorized access to do harm to the security of the US through espionage, terrorism, unauthorized disclosure of information, or through the loss or degradation of resources or capabilities."

It also establishes an inspection process to ensure that departments and agencies that handle national intelligence maintain effective operational security practices. Also in June 2012, the Office of the Director of National Intelligence announced two new measures aimed to protect classified information from unauthorized disclosure. The Director mandated the inclusion of a new question related to unauthorized disclosures to counterintelligence polygraph examinations and requested the Intelligence Community Inspector General to lead independent investigations of selected unauthorized disclosure cases where the Justice Department has declined to prosecute.[80]

The Department of Defense issued a revised version of the DOD Information Security Program manual, which among other things mandates a department-wide incident reporting system to track unauthorized disclosures. It also tasks the Undersecretary of Defense for Intelligence, in consultation with the Assistant Secretary for Public Affairs, with monitoring all "major, national level media reporting" for unauthorized disclosures of DOD classified information[81] as a part of a new "top down reporting system to detect unauthorized disclosures."

The Department also put into effect an automated security incident reporting system and an improved system for monitoring DOD networks, and initiated a DOD Insider Threat Program as well as an Unauthorized Disclosure Working Group.[82]

Congressional Activity

The 112th Congress held at least two hearings on the topic of unauthorized disclosures of classified information.[83] Congress also passed a measure as part of the National Defense Authorization Act for FY2012 to require the Defense Department to establish a "program for information sharing protection and insider threat mitigation for the information systems of the Department of Defense to detect unauthorized access to, use of, or transmission of classified or controlled unclassified information."[84] Its purpose appears to be avoidance of a reiteration of the *Wikileaks* disclosures, and the program is required to make use of both technology based solutions as well as a "governance structure and process" to integrate these technologies into existing security measures.

The Intelligence Authorization Act for FY2013, S. 3454, 112th Congress, as reported by the Senate Intelligence Committee, contained a number of measures to address the disclosure of classified information by federal employees, whether authorized or not, especially if the disclosure were to the media. Opposition to these measures resulted in a manager's amendment to the bill with all but one of these provisions removed.[85] Section 504 of the bill, as passed by both houses of Congress, requires a government official who approves a disclosure of classified information to the media, or to another person for publication, to first report the decision and other matters related to the disclosure to the congressional intelligence committees. The provision applies to "national intelligence or intelligence related to national security" that is classified or has been declassified for the purpose of making the disclosure, where the disclosure is made by a government officer, employee, or contractor. According to the original committee report, the reporting is intended to keep the intelligence committees apprised of expected media disclosures of relevant classified information and to assist in distinguishing between "authorized disclosures" and "unauthorized leaks."[86] As amended, the requirement sunsets one year after enactment.

Provisions that were dropped from the bill include a requirement for heads of agencies and departments of the intelligence community to maintain a list of all "authorized disclosures" to media personnel; a requirement to establish procedures for administrative investigations of unauthorized disclosures and to report the procedures and any investigations to the intelligence committees; a requirement for an assessment of measures to improve detection capabilities, including the practical feasibility of including questions regarding disclosure of classified information and contact with the media in polygraph examinations; and measures related to agency "insider threat" programs and employee non-disclosure agreements. Another provision would have required the Attorney General to submit a report to the congressional intelligence committees describing the effectiveness of and potential improvements to the process for investigating and prosecuting unauthorized disclosures of classified information; potential modifications to the policy on subpoenaing reporters; and suggested modifications to the Classified Information Procedures Act.[87]

Some of the more controversial measures that were eliminated from the bill involved restrictions on media access to government officials. One was a prohibition on federal officers, employees, and contractors who have security clearances, including some who have left government service within the prior year, from entering into agreements with the media to provide analysis or commentary on matters related to classified intelligence activities or intelligence related to national security. Another would have limited the individuals authorized to provide background or off-the-record information to the media regarding intelligence activities to the Director and Deputy Directors or their equivalents of each agency and designated public affairs officers. Another would have required the Director of National Intelligence to prescribe regulations regarding the interaction of cleared personnel with the media. Such persons would have been required to report all contacts with the media to the appropriate security office. Also eliminated was a prohibition on federal officers, employees, and contractors from possessing a security clearance after having made any unauthorized disclosure regarding the existence of, or classified details relating to, a covert action as defined in 50 U.S.C. Section 413(b).

End Notes

[1] See Harold Relyea, The Presidency and the People's Right to Know, in THE PRESIDENCY AND INFORMATION POLICY 1, 16-18 (1981).

[2] Exec. Order No. 8381 (1940).

[3] Compare Exec. Order No. 10501 (1953) with, e.g., Exec. Order No. 13292 (2003). The most recent Executive Order on classified information, Exec. Order No. 13526 (Dec. 29, 2009), also cites constitutional authority.

[4] U.S. CONST., art. II, §2.

[5] Department of the Navy v. Egan, 484 U.S. 518, 527 (1988) (quoting Cafeteria Workers v. McElroy, 367 U.S. 886, 890 (1961). In addition, courts have also been wary to second-guess the executive branch in areas of national security. See, e.g., Haig v. Agee, 453 U.S. 280, 291 (1981) ("Matters intimately related to foreign policy and national security are rarely proper subjects for judicial intervention."). The Court has suggested, however, that it might intervene where Congress has provided contravening legislation. Egan at 530 ("Thus, unless Congress specifically has provided otherwise, courts traditionally have been reluctant to intrude upon the authority of the Executive in military and national security affairs.")(emphasis added).

[6] EPA v. Mink, 410 U.S. 73, 83 (1973).

[7] 42 U.S.C. §2011 et seq. In addition, the Invention Secrecy Act (codified at 35 U.S.C. §181 et seq.) authorizes the Commissioner of Patents to keep secret those patents on inventions in which the government has an ownership interest and the widespread knowledge of which would, in the opinion of the interested agency, harm national security. For a more detailed discussion of these and other regulatory regimes for the protection of sensitive government information, see CRS Report RL33502, Protection of National Security Information, by Jennifer K. Elsea; CRS Report RL33303, "Sensitive But Unclassified" Information and Other Controls: Policy and Options for Scientific and Technical Information.

[8] Counterintelligence and Security Enhancement Act of 1994, Title VIII of P.L. 103-359 (codified at 50 U.S.C. §435 et seq.). Congress has also required specific regulations regarding personnel security procedures for employees of the National Security Agency, P.L. 88-290, 78 Stat. 168, codified at 50 U.S.C. §§831 - 835. Congress has also prohibited the Department of Defense from granting or renewing security clearances for officers, employees, or contract personnel who had been convicted of a crime (and served at least one year prison time) and for certain other reasons, with a waiver possible only in "meritorious cases," P.L. 106-398 §1, Div. A, Title X, §1071(a), 114 Stat. 1654, 10 U.S.C. §986.

[9] 50 U.S.C. §435(a).

[10] Id.

[11] Id. §435(b). The House Conference Report that accompanied this legislation in 1994 suggests that Congress understood that the line defining the boundaries of executive and legislative authority in this area is blurry at best. The conferees made explicit reference to the Egan case, expressing their desire that the legislation not be understood to affect the President's authority with regard to security clearances. See H.R. REP. 103-753, at 54.

[12] See Report of the Commission on Protecting and Reducing Government Secrecy, S. DOC. NO. 105-2, at 11 (1997).

[13] Id.

[14] See, e.g., Availability of Information from Federal Departments and Agencies: Hearings Before the House Committee on Government Operations, 85th Cong. (1955).

[15] 5 U.S.C. §552(b)(1). The Supreme Court has honored Congress's deference to executive branch determinations in this area. EPA v. Mink, 410 U.S. 73 (1973). Congress, concerned that the executive branch may have declared some documents to be "national security information" that were not vital to national security, added a requirement that such information be "properly classified pursuant to an executive order." 5 U.S.C. §552(b)(1)(B).

[16] P.L. 106-567, title VII, Dec. 27, 2000, 114 Stat. 2856, 50 U.S.C. §435 note.

[17] Id. §§705 and 707.

[18] P.L. 111-258, §6, codified at 50 U.S.C. §435 note.

[19] Classified National Security Information, Exec. Order No. 13526, 3 C.F.R. 298 (2009). For a more detailed description and analysis, see CRS Report R41528, Classified Information Policy and Executive Order 13526, by Kevin R. Kosar.

[20] Exec. Order No. 13526 §1.1. The unauthorized disclosure of foreign government information is presumed to damage national security. Id. §1.1(b).

[21] Id. §1.4. In addition, when classified information which is incorporated, paraphrased, restated, or generated in a new form, that new form must be classified at the same level as the original. Id. §§2.1 - 2.2.

[22] Id. §1.2.

[23] Id. Classifying authorities are specifically prohibited from classifying information for reasons other than protecting national security, such as to conceal violations of law or avoid embarrassment. Id. §1.7(a).

[24] Id. §§1.1-1.2. This presumption is a change from the predecessor order.

[25] Exec. Order No. 13526 at §1.5. Exceptions to the time guidelines are reserved for information that can be expected to reveal the identity of a human intelligence source or key design concepts of weapons of mass destruction. Id.

[26] Id. §1.5(c).

[27] Id. §3.1(a).

[28] Id. §3.1(d).

[29] Id. §3.3.

[30] 5 U.S.C. §552. For more information, see CRS Report R41406, The Freedom of Information Act and Nondisclosure Provisions in Other Federal Laws , by Gina Stevens.

[31] Exec. Order No. 13526 §3.5.

[32] 50 U.S.C. §§403-5c, 403-5e, 431.

[33] Exec. Order No. 13526 §3.5.

[34] Id. §3.4. "Need-to-know" is based on a determination within the executive branch in accordance with relevant directives that a prospective recipient "requires access to specific classified information in order to perform or assist in a lawful and authorized governmental function." Id. §6.1(dd).

[35] Id. §3.4. Exec. Order No. 13526 creates a new National Declassification Center (NDC) within the National Archives to facilitate and standardize the declassification process. Id. §3.7. For more information about the NDC, see CRS Report R41528, Classified Information Policy and Executive Order 13526, by Kevin R. Kosar.

[36] Id. §4.1.

[37] Id. §4.4.

[38] Id. §4.2.

[39] Id. §5.2.

[40] Id. §3.1(c).

[41] Id. §5.3.

[42] Id. §5.3(b)(1) - (3) For example, an authorized holder of classified information is allowed to challenge the classified status of such information if the holder believes that status is improper. Id. §1.8.

[43] Id. §5.5. Specifically, administrative sanctions available with respect to "officers and employees of the United States Government, and its contractors, licensees, certificate holders, and grantees" accused of violating government security regulations, "knowingly, willfully, or negligently," include "reprimand, suspension without pay, removal, termination of classification authority, loss or denial of access to classified information, or other sanctions in accordance with applicable law and agency regulation." See infra section "Civil Penalties and Other Measures."

[44] 46 Fed. Reg. 59,941 (1981), as amended by Exec .Order No. 13284, 68 Fed. Reg. 4,077 (2003), Exec. Order No. 13355, 69 Fed. Reg. 53,593 (2004) and Exec. Order No. 13470, 73 Fed. Reg. 45,328 (2008). A version of the Order as amended is available at http://www.fas.org/irp/offdocs/eo/eo-12333-2008.pdf.

[45] The Intelligence Community is defined by 50 U.S.C. § 401a(4) and E.O. 12333 to include the Office of the Director of National Intelligence (ODNI), the Central Intelligence Agency (CIA), the Bureau of Intelligence and Research of the Department of State (INR), the National Security Service of the Federal Bureau of Investigation (FBI), the Office of

Intelligence and Analysis of the Department of Homeland Security (DHS), the Office of Intelligence or the Coast Guard (CG), other DHS elements concerned with the analysis of intelligence information, the Office of Intelligence and Analysis of the Treasury Department, the Energy Department, the Drug Enforcement Agency (DEA), the Defense Intelligence Agency (DIA), the National Security Agency (NSA), the National Reconnaissance Office (NRO), the National Geospatial Intelligence Agency (NGA), Army Intelligence, Air Force Intelligence, Navy Intelligence, and Marine Corps Intelligence, as well as "[s]uch other elements of any other department or agency as may be designated by the President, or designated jointly by the Director of National Intelligence and the head of the department or agency concerned, as an element of the intelligence community."

[46] Available at http://www.dni.gov/files/documents/ICD/ICD_700.pdf.

[47] Available at http://www.fas.org/irp/dni/icd/icd-701.pdf.

[48] ICD 700 §D.3.c.

[49] Senior Officials of the Intelligence Community (SOICs) means "heads of departments and agencies with organizations in the Intelligence Community or the heads of such organizations." Exec. Order No. 12333 at §1.7.

[50] Available at http://www.dtic.mil/whs/directives/corres/pdf/521050p.pdf.

[51] The questions are listed in enclosure 4 of DoDD 5210.50, and apparently are part of a Memorandum of Understanding concluded between the Department of Justice and elements of the Intelligence Community. See U.S. Congress, Senate Select Committee on Intelligence, Concerning Unauthorized Disclosure of Classified Information, 106th Cong., 2nd sess., June 14, 2000 (Statement of Attorney General Janet Reno).

[52] For a broader overview of statutory provisions applicable to specific types of sensitive information, see CRS Report R41404, Criminal Prohibitions on the Publication of Classified Defense Information, by Jennifer K. Elsea.

[53] 18 U.S.C. §1924.

[54] 50 U.S.C. §783.

[55] 18 U.S.C. §798.

[56] 50 U.S.C. §421.

[57] "Classified information" for the purpose of this provision is defined as "information or material designated and clearly marked or clearly represented, pursuant to the provisions of a statute or Executive order (or a regulation or order issued pursuant to a statute or Executive order), as requiring a specific degree of protection against unauthorized disclosure for reasons of national security." 50 U.S.C. §426.

[58] See Department of Navy v. Egan, 484 U.S. 518, 526-29 (1988). Federal courts may review constitutional challenges based on the revocation of security clearance. Webster v. Doe, 486 U.S. 592 (1988).

[59] See 42 U.S.C. §2282(b) (providing for fine of up to $100,000 for violation of Department of Energy security regulations).

[60] 5 U.C.S. §8312 (2001)(listing violations of 18 U.S.C. §§793 & 798, 42 U.S.C. §2272-76, and 50 U.S.C. §421, among those for which forfeiture of retirement pay or annuities may be imposed).

[61] See United States v. Marchetti, 466 F.2d 1309 (4th Cir.), cert. denied, 409 U.S. 1063 (1972) (enforcing contractual non-disclosure agreement by former employee regarding "secret information touching upon the national defense and the conduct of foreign affairs" obtained through employment with CIA).

[62] See Snepp v. United States, 444 U.S. 507 (1980); see also Alan E. Garfield, Promises of Silence: Contract Law and Freedom of Speech, 83 CORNELL L. REV. 261, 274

(1998)(noting the remedy in Snepp was enforced despite the agency's stipulation that the book did not contain any classified information).

[63] See 18 U.S.C. §§793(h), 794(d), 798(d).

[64] 42 U.S.C. §2168(b).

[65] See United States v. Marchetti, 466 F.2d 1309 (4th Cir. 1972) (granting an injunction to prevent a former CIA agent from publishing a book disclosing government secrets).

[66] See Haig v. Agee, 453 U.S. 280 (1981).

[67] Declassification is an information management step that is distinct and precedes release. Thus, it is not unusual for information to be declassified and then a lengthy period ensues before it is publicly released.

[68] See National Security Leaks and the Law, Hearing before the Subcomm. on Crime, Terrorism and Homeland Security of the H. Comm. on the Judiciary 1-2, 112th Cong. (2012) (statement of Rep. Sensenbrenner).

[69] William S. Moorhead, Operation and Reform of the Classification System in the United States 90, in SECRECY AND FOREIGN POLICY (Thomas M. Franck and Edward Weisband, eds. 1974). For an account of notable government leaks at the time, see id. at at 89; Information Security: Classification of Government Documents, 85 HARV. L. REV. 1189, 1206-07 (1972). For a more recent chronology of government leaks, see Mary-Rose Papandrea, Lapdogs, Watchdogs, and Scapegoats: The Press and National Security Information, 83 IND. L.J. 233, 251-53 (2008) (quoting various high-level officials who admitted to leaking information in order to generate public support for a program or to promote some other political or bureaucratic agenda).

[70] E.O. 13,526 §1.2.

[71] "Unauthorized disclosure" means "a communication or physical transfer of classified information to an unauthorized recipient." Id. §6.1(rr). "Unauthorized" recipient is not defined.

[72] A person who does meet the criteria in Section 4.1.(a) is defined as an "authorized holder" under the definitions section of the Order, Section 6.1(c).

[73] 18 U.S.C. §793. For more information about criminal laws proscribing leaks, see CRS Report R41404, Criminal Prohibitions on the Publication of Classified Defense Information, by Jennifer K. Elsea. The level of knowledge required to prove an offense depends on the type of information alleged to have been disclosed, and it is not necessarily a crime to disclose information merely because it is classified. See id.

[74] Department of Defense, Department of Defense Manual, 5200.01-V3, February 24, 2012 encl. 6 at 93.

[75] Id. at 94.

[76] Exec. Order No. 13587, 3 C.F.R. 276 (2011), available at http://www.whitehouse.gov/the-press-office/2011/10/07/ executive-order-structural-reforms-improve-security-classified-networks-.

[77] Id. §6.

[78] Press Release, White House Office of the Press Secretary, Presidential Memorandum—National Insider Threat Policy and Minimum Standards for Executive Branch Insider Threat Programs (Nov. 21, 2012), available at http://www.whitehouse.gov/the-press-office/ 2012/11/21/presidential-memorandum-national-insider-threat-policy-andminimum-stand. The policy and standards do not appear to have been made public.

[79] Intelligence Community Directive (ICD) 700, Protection of National Intelligence, effective June 7, 2012, available at http://www.dni.gov/files/documents/ICD/ICD_700.pdf.

[80] Press Release, Office of the Director of National Intelligence, Director Clapper Announces Steps to Deter and Detect Unauthorized Disclosures (June 25, 2012), available at http://www.dni.gov/index.php/newsroom/press-releases/96- press-releases-2012/586-director-clapper-announces-steps-to-deter-and-detect-unauthorized-disclosures.

[81] Press Release, Department of Defense Office of the Assistant Secretary (Public Affairs), Statement from George Little on Defense Initiatives to Limit Unauthorized Disclosures of Classified Information (July 19, 2012), available at http://www.defense.gov/Releases/Release.aspx?ReleaseID=15451. The four-volume manual for the DOD Information Security Program is available at http://www.dtic.mil/whs/directives/corres/pub1.html.

[82] Id.

[83] National Security Leaks and the Law, Hearing before the Subcomm. on Crime, Terrorism and Homeland Security of the H. Comm. on the Judiciary, 112th Cong. (2012); Disclosures of National Security Information and Impact on Military Operations, Hearing before the H. Comm. on Armed Services, 112th Cong (2012).

[84] P.L. 112-81, §922, codified at 10 U.S.C. §2224 note.

[85] See Greg Miller, Senate Committee Drops Anti-Leaks Measures, WASH. POST, Dec. 22, 2012, at A3.

[86] S.Rept. 112-192.

[87] For information about the Classified Information Procedures Act, see CRS Report R41742, Protecting Classified Information and the Rights of Criminal Defendants: The Classified Information Procedures Act, by Edward C. Liu and Todd Garvey.

In: NSA Intelligence Collection, Leaks … ISBN: 978-1-62948-937-7
Editor: Simon Cepeda

Chapter 5

PROTECTION OF CLASSIFIED INFORMATION BY CONGRESS: PRACTICES AND PROPOSALS*

Frederick M. Kaiser

SUMMARY

The protection of classified national security and other controlled information is of concern not only to the executive branch—which, for the most part, determines what information is classified and controlled—but also to Congress. The legislature uses such information to fulfill its constitutional responsibilities, particularly overseeing the executive, appropriating funds, and legislating public policy. Congress has established numerous mechanisms to safeguard controlled information in its custody, although these arrangements have varied over time, between the two chambers, and among offices in each. Both chambers, for instance, have created offices of security to consolidate relevant responsibilities; but these were established nearly two decades apart. Other differences exist at the committee level, regarding the availability and use of information in committees' custody. Proposals for change, some of which are controversial and could be costly, usually seek to set uniform standards or heighten requirements for access.

---

* This is an edited, reformatted and augmented version of a Congressional Research Service publication, CRS Report for Congress RS20748, from www.crs.gov, dated August 31, 2011.

CURRENT PRACTICES AND PROCEDURES

Congress relies on a variety of mechanisms, instruments, and procedures to protect classified national security and other sensitive information in its custody.[1] Such information—most of which comes from the executive branch—can be hard to obtain. But accessibility to it is seen as necessary for the legislature to carry out its constitutional responsibilities, especially overseeing the executive and legislating public policy.

The safeguards surrounding information deal with who is eligible for access, what information is made available and in what form, where and when it can be accessed, and how and in what circumstances or contexts it can be used afterwards. The relevant requirements and mechanisms include

- House and Senate security offices responsible for setting and implementing standards for safeguarding classified information;
- committee rules determining access to committee-held classified information, including what is made available and to whom, as well as how and under what conditions;
- committee and certain chamber rules governing how classified information can be used afterwards, in what contexts and forums, and under what conditions;
- establishment of special congressional groups to receive highly sensitive classified information;
- a secrecy oath required for all Members and employees of the House and several of its committees;
- security clearances and nondisclosure agreements for staff; and
- formal procedures for investigating suspected security violations.

Public laws, House and Senate rules, and committee rules—as well as custom and practice, including informal agreements between legislators and executive officials—constitute the bases for these requirements and arrangements.[2] Some of these have evolved over time, in response to changing conditions and needs of both the legislative and executive branches.[3]

Chamber Offices of Security and Security Manuals

The two chambers have approached their security program differently, although each now has an office of security and a set of requirements, instructions, and guidelines regarding the protection of classified and other controlled information.

Senate

The Senate established an Office of Senate Security in 1987, the result of a bipartisan effort over two Congresses. It is charged with consolidating information and personnel security.[4] Located in the Office of the Secretary of the Senate, the Security Office sets and implements uniform standards for handling and safeguarding classified and other sensitive information in the Senate's possession. The Security Office's standards, procedures, and requirements—detailed in its *Senate Security Manual*, first issued in 1988—"are binding upon all employees of the Senate."[5] These cover committee and Member office staff and officers of the Senate as well as consultants and contract personnel—but not Members themselves. The regulations extend to a wide range of matters on safeguarding classified information: physical security requirements; procedures for storing materials; mechanisms for protecting communications equipment; security clearances and nondisclosure agreements for all Senate staff needing access; and follow-up investigations of suspected security violations by employees.

House

In 2005, the House put its own security office in place—the Office of House Security (OHS)— under the jurisdiction of the House Sergeant at Arms, following approval of the chamber's Committee on House Administration.6 The office, similar to the Senate predecessor, is charged with developing an Operations Security Program for the House. Its responsibilities and jurisdiction encompass processing security clearances for staff, handling and storing classified information, managing a counterintelligence program for the House, and coordinating security breach investigations.[7] Unlike its Senate counterpart, however, the House Office of Security has not issued an official security manual. Nonetheless, OHS provides relevant services, instructions, and forms for security clearances and other safeguards to protect classified information.[8] Prior to the establishment of OHS, the chamber had relied on individual committee and Member offices to set requirements following chamber and committee rules, guidelines in internal office procedural manuals, and custom.

Security Clearances and Nondisclosure Agreements for Staff

Although there is no across-the-board, comprehensive requirement for all legislative branch staff, they are required to have security clearances and written nondisclosure agreements to gain access to classified information. These exist through various mechanisms,[9] which apply to different employee categories:

House and Senate Committee Staff

Each panel spells out its requirements in its rules to cover access.[10] In addition, the Office of Senate Security and Office of House Security both require employees needing access to classified information to have security clearances and nondisclosure agreements in order to be eligible for access to classified national security information.[11] A provision in the *Senate Security Manual* along these lines stipulates that "Senators and Committee Chairmen must determine which positions on their staffs require a security clearance. Clearances will only be granted to employees whose assignments require access to classified information."[12]

House and Senate Member Office Staff

Individual Member offices may on their own require both clearances and nondisclosure agreements for staff to be eligible for access. Even so, requirements and limitations are directed by each chamber's office of security.[13] A limit may also be imposed on the number of staff with clearances in any individual Member office.[14] Along with this, congressional offices may on their own require a need-to-know for individual staffers seeking access to certain classified information.

Legislative Branch Support Agencies

Security clearance requirements are included in the personnel manuals, job and position descriptions, or vacancy announcements of Congress's support agencies: Congressional Budget Office (CBO), Congressional Research Service (CRS) as well as the Library of Congress (LOC), and Government Accountability Office (GAO).[15]

Secrecy Oaths for Members and Staff

The House and Senate differ with regard to secrecy oaths for Members and staff. Neither the full Senate nor any Senate panel apparently imposes a secrecy oath or affirmation on its Members or employees.

The House, by comparison, has adopted such special procedures. Beginning with the 104th Congress, the House has required a secrecy oath (taken once per Congress) for each Member, Delegate, Resident Commissioner, officer, and employee of the chamber. Before any such person may have access to classified information, he or she must

> solemnly swear (or affirm) that I will not disclose any classified information received in the course of my service with the House of Representatives, except as authorized by the House of Representatives or in accordance with its Rules.[16]

Previously, a similar oath was required only for Members and staff of the House Permanent Select Committee on Intelligence. This requirement had been added in the 102nd Congress as part of the select committee's internal rules, following abortive attempts to establish it in public law.[17] The oath is still in effect for the panel's Members and staff:

> I do solemnly swear (or affirm) that I will not disclose or cause to be disclosed any classified information received in the course of my service on the House Permanent Select Committee on Intelligence, except when authorized to do so by the Committee or the House of Representatives.[18]

At least one other panel has adopted a similar measure. The House Committee on Homeland Security requires an oath or affirmation from each committee Member or staff seeking access to classified information, modeled after the one adopted by the House Intelligence Committee.[19]

Sharing Committee-Held Information with Non-Committee Members

Procedures controlling access to classified information held by congressional offices exist throughout Congress. Although these differ, committee and chamber rules set conditions and requirements for sharing such information with other panels, Members, and staff.[20] This includes determining:

- who may attend a panel's executive (or secret) session hearings;
- who is eligible for access to a committee's classified holdings;
- what information may be made available to all Members across-the-board; and if so, how, to what extent, and in what form;[21]
- what specific committee-held information is to be made available to non-committee Members seeking access; a panel's requirements and conditions for access may depend on what the information covers (the specific subject matter and a need-to-know), to what extent it may be made available (all or only a part of it), in what form (e.g., the actual documents, a summary account, or a briefing from a committee Member or staff), under what restrictions (with or without staff in attendance or taking notes), or where (in the committee offices, most likely, or in a secure area elsewhere); and
- how and in what other forums (e.g., with another congressional panel or on the floor of the chamber) may the information be used and under what restrictions.

The most exacting requirements along these lines have been developed by the House Permanent Select Committee on Intelligence; its rules are based on the committee's 1977 establishing authority and reinforced by intelligence oversight provisions in public law, such as the 1991 Intelligence Authorization Act.[22] The panel's controls apply to select committee Members sharing classified information outside the committee itself as well as to non-committee Representatives seeking access to the panel's holdings.[23] In the latter case, an individual requester must go through a multi-stage process to obtain access.[24] Consequently, it is possible for a non-committee Member to be denied attendance at its executive sessions or access to its classified holdings; given only a briefing on it; granted partial access; or allowed full access. The select committee also sets rules on whether the Member may be accompanied by a cleared staffer or may take notes. When the House Select Committee on Intelligence releases classified information to another panel or non-member, moreover, the recipient must comply with the same rules and procedures that govern the intelligence committee's control and disclosure requirements.[25]

By comparison, rules of the House Armed Services Committee are to "ensure access to information [classified at Secret or higher] by any member of the Committee or any other Member, Delegate, or Resident Commissioner of the House of Representatives ... who has requested the opportunity to review such material."[26]

Limiting Access to Special Groups: The "Gang of Eight" and "Gang of Four"

Executive branch notification about intelligence activities, including presidential findings regarding covert operations, is usually provided directly to the House and Senate select committees on intelligence.

These full panels, however, may be bypassed—based on the urgency of a situation, to meet extraordinary circumstances affecting the vital interests of the United States, or to protect the extremely sensitive nature of the information—in favor of notification to the so-called "Gang of Eight" or "Gang of Four."[27] Notification about covert operations, in certain situations, is submitted to the statute-based "Gang of Eight," composed of the Speaker and minority leader of the House and chairman and ranking minority Member of its intelligence committee and the majority and minority leaders of the Senate and chairman and vice chairman of its intelligence committee. A separate so-called "Gang of Four" has also come into existence to receive briefings on particularly sensitive intelligence activities (other than covert operations), which, if disclosed, might reveal intelligence sources and methods. This non-statutory body is composed of the chairs and ranking minority Members of the House and Senate select committees on intelligence. On occasion, its meetings are attended by their staff directors.

A controversy had erupted recently, however, over the existing arrangements, when the intelligence committees are not the direct and immediate recipients of these presidential findings or executive briefings. The dispute arose, in part, because the members of either "Gang" had not been permitted to share the information with the full intelligence committee in their respective chamber; and they may have been delayed or prevented from even informing their panel that a notification or briefing had occurred.

The primary response by Congress was to modify the notification procedures—via the Intelligence Authorization Act of FY2010—allowing for more communication between the members of the "Gangs" and their respective select committees on intelligence.[28] Such new congressional notification procedures, along with several other proposed changes in the law, however, were of "serious concern to the Intelligence Community," prompting a threatened presidential veto.[29] (A veto did not materialize.) The executive's opposition had been based on the changes' perceived adverse impact on "the long tradition of comity between the branches regarding intelligence matters."[30]

Investigation of Security Breaches

The Senate Office of Security and the House counterpart are charged with investigating or coordinating investigations of suspected security violations by employees.[31] In addition, investigations by the House and Senate Ethics Committees of suspected breaches of security are authorized by each chamber's rules, directly and indirectly. The Senate Ethics Committee, importantly, has the broad duty to "receive complaints and investigate allegations of improper conduct which may reflect upon the Senate, violations of law, violations of the Senate Code of Official Conduct, and violations of rules and regulations of the Senate."[32] The panel is also directed "to investigate any unauthorized disclosure of intelligence information [from the Senate Intelligence Committee] by a Member, officer or employee of the Senate."[33] The House, in creating its Permanent Select Committee on Intelligence, issued similar instructions. H.Res. 658 ordered the Committee on Standards of Official Conduct to "investigate any unauthorized disclosure of intelligence or intelligence-related information [from the House Intelligence Committee] by a Member, officer, or employee of the House."[34]

Other Protective Measures

In addition to the foregoing, each chamber and its committees subscribe to other measures designed to protect classified and controlled information. Some of these—derived from the House and Senate Offices of Security or such committees as the House and Senate select committees on intelligence—focus on the physical security of documents and facilities, while others affect individual conduct. These include

- stationing U.S. Capitol Police officers at committee sites;
- conducting Technical Security Countermeasures sweeps of offices and facilities to detect surveillance devices (e.g., bugs) and technical security weaknesses;
- safeguarding the storage and use of controlled information;

- setting up procedures to acknowledge the receipt of specific classified information and its dissemination to particular individuals;
- conducting education and training programs; and
- reporting foreign travel and foreign national contact.

PROPOSALS FOR CHANGE

A variety of proposals—coming from congressional bodies, government commissions, and other groups—have called for changes in the procedures for handling and safeguarding classified information in the custody of Congress.[35] These plans, some of which might be controversial or costly, focus on setting uniform standards for congressional offices and employees and heightening access eligibility requirements.

Mandate That Members of Congress Hold Security Clearances to Be Eligible for Access to Classified Information

This would mark a significant and unprecedented departure from the past. Members of Congress (as with the President and Vice President, Justices of the Supreme Court, or other federal court judges) have never been required to hold security clearances. Most of the proposals along this line appeared in the late 1980s, following charges and countercharges between the executive and legislative branches over unauthorized disclosure of classified information. A more recent bill, introduced in 2006, would have required a security clearance for Members serving on the House Permanent Select Committee on Intelligence and on the Subcommittee on Defense of the House Appropriations Committee.[36] The resolution, however, did not specify which entity (in the legislative or executive branch) would conduct the background investigation or which officer (in Congress or in the executive) would adjudicate the clearances of Members.

The broad mandate for such clearances could be applied to four different groups: (1) all Senators and Representatives, thus, in effect, becoming a condition for serving in Congress; (2) only Members seeking access to classified information, including those on the panels receiving it; (3) only Members on committees which receive classified information; or (4) only those seeking access to classified information held by panels where they are not members.

Under a security clearance requirement, background investigations might be conducted by an executive branch agency, such as the Office of Personnel Management or Federal Bureau of Investigation; by a legislative branch entity, such as the House or Senate Office of Security, or the Government Accountability Office; or possibly by a private investigative firm under contract. Possible adjudicators—that is, the officials who would judge, based on the background investigation, whether applicants would be "trustworthy" and, therefore, eligible for access to classified information—could extend to the majority or minority leaders, a special panel in each chamber, a chamber officer, or even an executive branch officer, if Congress so directed.

Pros

The main goals behind this proposed change are to tighten and make uniform standards governing eligibility for access for Members. Proponents maintain that it would help safeguard classified information by ensuring access only by Members deemed "trustworthy" and, thereby, limit the possibility of leaks and inadvertent disclosures. In addition, the clearance process itself might make recipients more conscious of and conscientious about the need to safeguard this information as well as the significance attached to it. As a corollary, supporters might argue that mandating a clearance to serve on a panel possessing classified information could increase its members' appreciation of the information's importance and its protection's priority. This, in turn, might help the committee members gain the access to information that the executive is otherwise reluctant to share and improve comity between the branches.

Cons

Opponents, by contrast, contend that security clearance requirements would compromise the independence of the legislature if an executive branch agency conducted the background investigation, had access to the information it generated, or adjudicated the clearance. Even if the process were fully under legislative control, concerns might arise over a number of matters: its fairness, impartiality, objectivity, and correctness (if determined by an inexperienced person); the effects of a negative judgment on a Member, both inside and outside Congress; and the availability of information gathered in the investigation—which may not be accurate or substantiated—to other Members or to another body, such as the chamber's ethics committee or Justice Department, if it is seen as incriminating in matters of ethics or criminality.

Opponents might also contend that adding this new criterion could have an adverse impact on individual Members, the full legislature, and the legislative process in other ways. It might impose an unnecessary, unprecedented, and unique (among elected federal officials and members of the federal judiciary) demand on legislators; create two classes of legislators, those with or without a clearance; affect current requirements for non-Member access to holdings of committees whose own members might need clearances; possibly jeopardize participation by Members without clearances in floor or committee proceedings (even secret sessions); and inordinately slow down the legislative process, while background investigations, adjudications, and appeals connected with security clearances of Members are conducted.

Direct Senators or Senate Employees to Take or Sign a Secrecy Oath to Be Eligible for Access

This proposal would require a secrecy oath for Senators and staffers, similar to the current requirement for their House counterparts. An earlier attempt to mandate such an oath for all Members and employees of both chambers of Congress seeking access to classified information arose in 1993, but it was unsuccessful.[37] If approved, it would have prohibited intelligence entities from providing classified information to Members of Congress and their staff, as well as officers and employees of the executive branch, unless the recipients had signed a nondisclosure agreement. Each would have to pledge that he or she "will not willfully directly or indirectly disclose to any unauthorized person any classified information"—and the oath had been published in the *Congressional Record*.[38]

Direct All Cleared Staff—or Just Those Cleared for the Highest Levels—to File Financial Disclosure Statements Annually

This demand might make it easier to detect and investigate possible misconduct instigated for financial reasons. And many staff with high-level clearances may already file financial disclosure statements, because of their employment rank or salary level; consequently, few new costs would be added. Nonetheless, objections might arise because the proposal would impose yet another burden on staff and result in additional record-keeping and costs. This requirement's effectiveness in preventing leaks or espionage might also be questioned by opponents.

Require Polygraph Examinations and/or Drug Tests for Staff to Be Eligible for Access to Classified Information

Under such proposals, drug tests or polygraph examinations could be imposed in several different circumstances: as a condition of employment for all personnel in offices holding classified information, only on staff seeking access to such information, or for both employment and access. Objections have been expressed to such tests, especially as a pre-condition of employment, however, because of their costs and questioned reliability and validity.[39]

End Notes

[1] Classification of national security information (and eligibility for access to it in the executive branch) is governed by executive orders, public laws, and administrative directives. For coverage of this issue, see CRS Report RL33494, *Security Classified and Controlled Information: History, Status, and Emerging Management Issues*, by Kevin R. Kosar; and CRS Report RS21900, *The Protection of Classified Information: The Legal Framework*, by Jennifer K. Elsea.

[2] A number of CRS reports deal with various aspects of this area: CRS Report R40136, *Congress as a Consumer of Intelligence Information*, by Alfred Cumming and Richard A. Best Jr.; CRS Report R40691, *Sensitive Covert Action Notifications: Oversight Options for Congress*, by Alfred Cumming and Richard A. Best Jr.; CRS Report R40698, *"Gang of Four" Congressional Intelligence Notifications*, by Alfred Cumming and Richard A. Best Jr.; CRS Report RL32525, *Congressional Oversight of Intelligence: Current Structure and Alternatives*, by Frederick M. Kaiser; CRS Report R40602; *The Department of Homeland Security Intelligence Enterprise: Operational Overview and Oversight Challenges for Congress*, by Jerome P. Bjelopera; CRS Report RL33616, *Homeland Security Intelligence: Perceptions, Statutory Definitions, and Approaches*, by Mark A. Randol; and CRS Report RL30240, *Congressional Oversight Manual*, by Frederick M. Kaiser, Walter J. Oleszek, and Todd B. Tatelman, especially pp. 61-69.

[3] For further background on the protection of classified information by Congress, see Frederick M. Kaiser, "Congressional Rules and Conflict Resolution: Access to Information in the House Select Committee on Intelligence," *Congress and the Presidency*, vol. 15 (1988), pp. 49-73; U.S. Commission on Protecting and Reducing Government Secrecy, *Secrecy: Report of the Commission* (1997); House Committee on Government Operations, Subcommittee on Legislation and National Security, *Congress and the Administration's Secrecy Pledges*,

Hearings, 100th Cong., 2nd sess. (1988); House Permanent Select Committee on Intelligence, *United States Counterintelligence and Security Concerns—1986*, 100th Cong., 1st sess., H. Rept. 100-5 (1987), pp. 3-4; Joint Committee on the Organization of Congress, *Committee Structure*, Hearings, 103rd Cong., 1st sess. (1993), pp. 64-79, 312-316, 406-417, and 832-841; Senate Select Committee on Intelligence, *Meeting the Espionage Challenge*, S. Rept. 99-522, 99th Cong., 2nd sess. (1986), pp. 90-95; and Office of the Director of National Intelligence, *Reporting of Intelligence Activities to Congress*, Intelligence Community Policy Memorandum Number 2005-100-3 (10 Jan. 06), and *Reforming Intelligence: The Passage of the Intelligence Reform and Terrorism Prevention Act* (Washington: ODNI, 2008).

[4] *Congressional Record*, vol. 133, July 1, 1987, pp. 18506-18507. The resolution creating the new office (S.Res. 243, 100th Cong.) was introduced and approved on the same day.

[5] U.S. Senate, Office of Senate Security (OSS), *Security Manual* (revised, 2007), preface.

[6] The two relevant letters—one requesting an Operations Security Program under the direction of the House Sergeant at Arms and the other granting approval—are, respectively, to the Chairman of the House Committee on House Administration, from the House Sergeant at Arms, February 25, 2003; and to the House Sergeant at Arms, from the Chairman of the House Committee on House Administration, March 28, 2003.

[7] These are derived from its establishing authority (ibid.) and spelled out in House Office of the Sergeant at Arms, Office of House Security, *OHS Website*, available at http://saa.house.gov/ohs, and *Security Clearances*, available at http://saa.house.gov/ohs/security-clearances.

[8] Ibid.

[9] Herrick S. Fox, "Staffers Find Getting Security Clearances Is Long and Often a Revealing Process," *Roll Call*, October 30, 2000, pp. 24-25.

[10] For examples, see U.S. House Permanent Select Committee on Intelligence, *Rules of Procedure*, 112th Congress, Rules 12(b) and 14(c); and House Committee on Homeland Security, *Committee Rules*, 112th Congress, Rule XV(C).

[11] OSS, *Security Manual*, pp. 8 and 10; and OHS, *Security Clearances*.

[12] OSS, *Security Manual*, p. 8.

[13] Ibid. and OHS, *Security Clearances*.

[14] Only two cleared staff, for instance, are allotted to an individual House Member's office at any one time. OHS, *Security Clearances*.

[15] For illustration, see CBO, *Employment Opportunities*, "Employment Requirements," available at https://careers.cbo.gov/ext/search.asp; CRS and LOC, Office of the Inspector General, LOC, *Office of Security and Emergency Preparedness: Survey of the Personnel Security Office's Policies and Procedures*, Audit Survey Report No. 2011-PA-102 (Washington, DC, 2011), p.5; and GAO, position description for Controller, Administrative Service Officer (SES Career Appointment), available at http://jobview.usajobs.gov/GetJob.aspx?JobIG=101883709&JobTitle=Controller%2Ad.

[16] House Rule XXIII, cl. 13, 112th Congress. Copies of the oath or affirmation are retained by the Clerk as part of the records of the House. Ibid.

[17] U.S. Congress, Committee of Conference, *Intelligence Authorization Act, Fiscal Year 1992*, 102nd Cong., 1st sess., H. Rept. 102-327 (Washington: GPO, 1991), pp. 35-36.

[18] House Intelligence Committee, *Rules of Procedure*, Rule 14(d).

[19] U.S. House Committee on Homeland Security, *Committee Rules*, 112th Congress, Rule XV(E).

[20] For further discussion, see the citations in footnote 2, above.

[21] For example, the classified annex to the annual intelligence authorization act is available to Members in the secure offices of the select committees on intelligence. Committees may also selectively release classified information to Members of their own chamber. As an illustration, see Hon. Silvestre Reyes, Chairman, House Permanent Select Committee on Intelligence, Dear Colleague letter regarding access to two classified Central Intelligence Agency reports, March 13, 2009. Based on a request from a select committee member and approved by the panel, these reports were made "available to all members of the House who have executed the [standard] secrecy oath .... and who will be asked to sign a specific non-disclosure agreement." Ibid.

[22] H.Res. 658, 95th Congress; and P.L. 102-88, 105 Stat. 441. For background, see Kaiser, "Congressional Rules and Conflict Resolution."

[23] House Intelligence Committee, *Rules*, Rules 13(b) and 14(f).

[24] Ibid., Rule 14(f).

[25] Ibid., Rule 14(f)(4)(B).

[26] U.S. House Committee on Armed Services, *Rules of the Committee, 112th Congress*, Rule 20(b). The same provision applies to committee staff, along with one individual of each committee Member's personal staff (designated by the Member in a letter to the committee chair and approved by the chair) "who have the appropriate security clearances and the need to know." Ibid., Rules 20(b) and 9(c).

[27] For coverage of these select groups and related matters, see CRS reports by Cumming and Best cited in footnote 2.

[28] P.L. 111-259, sec. 331.

[29] Peter R. Orszag, Director, Office of Management and Budget, letter to Hon. Dianne Feinstein and Hon. Silvestre Reyes, regarding the Intelligence Authorization Act for Fiscal Year 2010, and *Conference Letter regarding S. 1494 and H.R. 2701, the Intelligence Authorization Act for Fiscal Year 2010*, p. 1.

[30] Orszag, *Conference Letter*, p. 1. The *Conference Letter* continues: these changes would "undermine this fundamental compact between the Congress and the President regarding the reporting of sensitive intelligence matters as embodied in Title V of the National Security Act—an arrangement that for decades has balanced congressional oversight responsibilities with the President's responsibility to protect sensitive national security information." Ibid.

[3]1 For Senate staff, see OSS, *Security Manual*, pp. 10-11, which spells out the investigative procedures and penalties for violations.

[32] S.Res. 388, 88th Congress.

[33] S.Res. 400, 94th Congress.

[34] H.Res. 658, 95th Congress.

[35] See citations in footnote 2, above.

[36] H.Res. 747, 109th Congress.

[37] *Congressional Record*, daily ed., vol. 139, Aug. 4, 1993, pp. H5770-H5773; and Nov. 18, 1993, p. H10157.

[38] Ibid.

[39] For background on polygraph testing, see CRS Congressional Distribution Memorandum, *Polygraph Examinations of Federal Employees and Applicants*, by Frederick M. Kaiser; and CRS Report RL31988, *Polygraph Use by the Department of Energy: Issues for Congress*, by Alfred Cumming.

INDEX

D

E

F

S

T

V

W

Y